Zero Percent Chance

What do you do when there is nothing you can do?

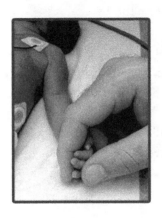

Zero Percent Chance.
What do you do when there is nothing you can do?
© 2023 by Blake Hamby
All rights reserved. No part of this book may be reproduced, stored in a retrieval system, or transmitted in any form or by any means—for example, electronic, mechanical, photocopy, recording, or otherwise—without the publisher's prior written permission or by license agreement. The only exception is brief quotations in printed reviews.

The author is not engaged in rendering medical or psychological services, and this book in not intended as a guide to diagnose or treat medical or psychological problems. If medical, psychological, or other expert assistance is required, the reader should seek the services of a health-care provider or certified counselor. This book is not intended to replace or alter the advice of health or mental health care professionals.

The events and conversations in this book have been set down to the best of the author's ability, although some names and details have been changed to protect the privacy of individuals.

All Scripture quotations, unless otherwise indicated, are taken from the Holy Bible, New International Version®, NIV®. Copyright ©1973, 1978, 1984, 2011 by Biblica, Inc.™ Used by permission of Zondervan. All rights reserved worldwide. www.zondervan.com. The "NIV" and "New International Version" are trademarks registered in the United States Patent and Trademark Office by Biblica, Inc.™

Pictures/courtesy of Blake & Erin Hamby, Zion Media, LLC
Design, Formatting, and Publishing by Zion Media, LLC
ISBN 979-8-9888588-0-5, print
ISBN 979-8-9888588-1-2, epub
ISBN 979-8-9888588-2-9, audiobook
Printed in the United States of America
23 24 25 26 27 28 29 30 31 / 5 4 3 2 1

Dedicated to Foster
and
all those who have lost loved
ones well before their time

Contents

Dedication / iii
Prologue / 21

Chapter One
Clean Sheets / 25

Chapter Two
Misdirection / 33

Chapter Three
Unremembering / 43

Chapter Four
Turbulence / 55

Chapter Five
Sh!%ty Situations / 69

Chapter Six
Familiar Things That Are Unfamiliar / 77

Chapter Seven
Mountains / 81

Chapter Eight
Zero Percent Chance / 87

Chapter Nine
Birthdays / 99

Chapter Ten
Meaning / 113

Chapter Eleven
Encouragers / 123

Chapter Twelve
Nightmares / 133

Chapter Thirteen
It's A Wonderful Life / 141

Chapter Fourteen
Christmas / 149

Chapter Fifteen
Moving On / 153

Chapter Sixteen
Familiar Places / 157

Chapter Seventeen
Game Time / 163

Chapter Eighteen
First Impressions / 171

Chapter Nineteen
Saran Wrap / 179

Chapter Twenty
National Champions / 187

Chapter Twenty-One
Mama Elephants / 191

Chapter Twenty-Two
CaringBridge / 197

Chapter Twenty-Three
Good Trouble / 211

Chapter Twenty-Four
Round and Round / 221

Chapter Twenty-Five
Dreams / 229

Chapter Twenty-Six
Elevators / 233

Chapter Twenty-Seven
Failure to Thrive / 241

Chapter Twenty-Eight
Burdens / 247

Chapter Twenty-Nine
Ventilator / 251

Chapter Thirty
Disney World / 259

Chapter Thirty-One
Days Revisited / 263

Chapter Thirty-Two
Losing My Mind / 271

Chapter Thirty-Three
Beatitudes / 279

Chapter Thirty-Four
Dark Places / 287

Chapter Thirty-Five
Old Friends / 291

Chapter Thirty-Six
Skin to Skin / 295

Chapter Thirty-Seven
Home / 303

Chapter Thirty-Eight
Legacy / 307

Chapter Thirty-Nine
Poker / 319

Chapter Forty
Sisters / 327

Chapter Forty-One
Lost / 335

Chapter Forty-Two
Hope / 339

Chapter Forty-Three
Even If / 349

Chapter Forty-Four
You / 361

Chapter Forty-Five
Faith / 367

THANK YOU

Writing a book is hard.

Getting a book from a final draft to what you actually hold in your hands might be even harder. Our hats go off to all those who do this as a profession. We hold a new respect for the works this takes!

Through our journey to get to this point there are truly countless people to thank and we will undoubtedly miss some through these next several paragraphs, but this is our attempt to try and cover as many as we can. Maybe it is because I am from Alabama and love Alabama football, but I feel most things in life can be related back to football. When I think about how we find ourselves at the closing seconds of bringing a book to market, I know we would never had made it without a strong team. If we were building a football team, we believe the roster below would be the odds on favorite to stand at the end of the season and lift the national championship trophy.

HEAD COACH – JESUS:

The head coach has the ultimate say. The head coach is the one who calls the shots. It is the joy of my life to have Jesus as my coach. I for sure do not want me calling the shots or having the final say. Without Jesus, I am probably sitting in a ditch somewhere or worse. I truly owe my life to Him. Jesus has been Ephesians 3:20-21 for me in every bright and dark place in my life for over 20 years. We say to Him be the glory throughout all generations, forever!

ASSISTANT COACHES - FAMILY:

Every great team has a staff that helps to carry out the vision of the head coach. There are different coaches for different positions, all with the same goal of making the team the best it can be. That diversity of insight and expertise is critical to a well balanced team. Each person in both my immediate and extended family has served as a specific coach for me in one way or another to help me become a more well balanced person.

Thank You

Words cannot express the thankfulness I feel for my wife Erin. You make me better in so many ways. This story is obvious your story and without your strength and your faith there is no story. This is my attempt to give the world a small glimpse of what I get to see each and every day. My life is not just better, but more EXCITING because I am your husband. I love you.

Next, our two amazing girls. As Mom says often, you are our Angel and our Miracle. We get the joy of having a front row seat to watching you grow from young girls, into young ladies. It is the joy of our lives to be on this journey with you. You truly make us proud to be known as your parents.

And to our extended family. We say it often, but it is so true, WE LOVE OUR FAMILY! You all love us so well and make our lives so much richer. Each of you loved us on through this journey and we are forever thankful for each of you. You all have shown me the blessing of Joshua 24:15. I am forever grateful for you choosing wisely who you will serve.

OFFENSE - THE PUBLISHING TEAM:

If the offense can not move the ball down the field, it is going to be hard to find the end zone. Strong offenses are also fun to watch. Every sports fan knows the excitement of seeing your team advance the ball down the field. Our offensive lineup took what seemed like an impossible dream and allowed it to move down the field. They never stopped believing with us and their skills allowed us to finally reach the end zone. And it was fun doing it with them! Below is our starting lineup.

Molly Venzke. We truly would not be here without you. You took us on as a project and believed in us when we were struggling to get past a bunch of jumbled ideas in a Word document. You have been a constant throughout this process and your guidance, encouragement and knowledge are sprinkled over all these pages. In addition to being our constant cheerleader, you were also our coach who was never afraid to give us your honest feedback to try and make this project the best it could be.

Julie Cantrell. You came into the process at just the right time. Your easy manner made us feel comfortable from the start. You took our book and polished off the rough edges. You examined every word and made them shine brighter than we ever could. We are grateful Lauren introduced us and know that this book is better because you were willing to get involved.

Janyre Tromp: We knew from our first conversation that the Lord brought us together on this project. Similar experiences make for quick connections and we felt that with you. You examined our words and helped make my lack of attention in English class less evident. We are grateful you where willing to work with us and feel more confident in our finished project.

Colin Edwards: You were the perfect person to step into this process to bring it over the finish line. Your perpetual positivity is so refreshing. You exude gratefulness and joy. When we felt like we might have a story that we could never get over the finish line because the publishing process seemed to be a mystery hidden in a riddle that could only be cracked if we had a "platform" and thousands of followers on social media, you showed up. You have great insight into what it takes to bring stories to the market. We are so grateful Scott introduced us. You and Lauren are a gift to many.

Each of you, and others, brought to life 2 Chronicles 15: 7. You all were strong and never gave up.

DEFENSE - THE MEDICAL TEAM:

Every lover of sports knows if you can keep your opponent from scoring points, your chances of winning increase dramatically. When you tune into your favorite team on a fall Saturday you want to see some of the fiercest men standing on the other side of the ball striking fear into the opposing team. You want them to know if they get an inch, they are going to have to go through hell to get it. The medical team was that defense for us. When medical issues beyond our understanding or control tried to gain ground, the medical professionals were lined up ready to fight back with everything they had. So we don't find ourselves in HIPPA jail we will not mention the many medical professionals by name. Plus, there are too many to thank on this platform. But we know that we would not be sitting here without their caring hearts, knowledge and dedication to helping strangers through their most trying times. We wish we could go back now, after all these years and find each of you and let you know we don't go very long without feeling a sense of gratitude rise up inside us for what you did for us all those years ago.

Each of the medical staff added flesh and bone to 2 Timothy 4:18. We know God works through people and gave each of you wisdom, knowledge and skill to rescue us from every evil attack.

SPECIAL TEAMS - FRIENDS:

Football games have been won and lost due to special teams. As an Alabama fan, I can still hear the chant of Punt Bama Punt. And I will never forget watching Auburn run back a short field goal attempt with one second left in the now infamous, "Kick Six". To our friends who showed up in so many ways, we thank you. The seemingly insi nificant text, was anything but insignificant. The food brought to our hospital room provided more than physical nourishment. The prayers you prayed over us gave us the fuel to lite the fire of hope that so often tried to go out. Each of you truly changed the game for us. When we thought we had no time left, you came onto the field, believing there was still hope. You gave us the truth of Ecclesiastes 4: 10. We feel down many times, but we always had our friends to help us back up.

FANS – CARING BRIDGE VISITORS

Every sports team is better because of their fans. Fans can actually help swing the momentum of what happens on the field. The 520 people who visited our journal page on Caring Bridge did this for us. You showed up in what could have seemed like an insignificant role, but it was anything but that. To each of the 520 visitors who took time out of your day to come to our site, this book is for you. We would not be here without you and we would not have written this book without you.

The first iteration of this book was simply to reformat the posts and your comments! While we would have loved to do that, it probably would not have the mass appeal we are hoping for… But the heart behind that has never changed. You all gave us the medicine no one else could. You gave us hope. We could not have sustained ourselves without it. We would love to find each of you and give you a hug and let you know how much you matter. The cheers you gave us helped us to push through in those times when we did not think we could play another down. You showed us the truth of Hebrews 12:1. We felt so surrounded by such a great cloud of witness who never tired of cheering us on so we could run our race with perseverance.

Author's Note

What do you when there is nothing you can do?

It is a question we will all face in some way during our lives. Whether it is a situation that has no answer or a situation that only has bad answers, none of us will be exempt from facing these realities.

To be clear, I am not here to tell you that I have answers to these hard questions. I don't. But I do have a story that helped me find something that I believe is more important than the question. That is more important than an outcome.

Because the truth is, not all stories end in outcomes that are pleasant. Or fun. And spoken quite plainly, the outcomes of some stories are simply unfair. We don't live in a Hollywood world where we get to wrap everything neatly together at the end. We live in a messy world that can be cruel and unfair at times. Why does one person get the dream date to the prom and another stays home alone and lonely? Why does one person with plenty get the promotion when another gets terminated while trying to figure out how to put food on the table? Why does one person leave the hospital with loved ones and another never leaves at all?

These are not fun questions. But if we are being honest, I believe they are questions each of us struggle to find appropriate answers to. And honestly, the story I have tried to tell that helped me find my something that is bigger than all those ugly questions is not really my story at all. It is my wife's story. My daughter's story. My family's story. The story I have tried to tell is one that highlights what friends and strangers did for us when we could not do them ourselves. The story of medical professionals and janitors that delivered healing in vastly different ways, but in equally critical ways. However, after many discussions with people smarter than me and a lot of prayer this is the story that came out. And I guess I just have to trust it is the story that was supposed to be told. And if I have done my job well, the story you read will be about all those people. Because they truly are the heartbeat of this story. I guess someone just needed to tell it.

Take this journey with me. See if you find something in these people that is bigger than your situation that you can cling to in your dark days when the question is asked of you, "What do you do when there is nothing you can do?"

Blake Hamby
Birmingham, AL

Prologue

December 17, 2011

What if I just backed out of the hospital parking lot, stopped at the gas station, bought a six-pack, put in my Willie Nelson box set, and drove West? Surely far away was a place where I could feel whole again. Useful again. A place where I could regain my strength and hold things together. A place where all hope was not lost. A place where Doctors did not say that our baby has a "zero percent chance of surviving."

When I'd heard those words, I'd immediately felt as cold as the tile floor of the hospital room where my wife was confined. Growing up in rural Alabama, I hadn't spent much time studying advanced mathematics, but I did know that zero times anything else equals zero. In my simple mind I realized the declaration of "zero percent chance" was not just something a very educated and experienced doctor had told us, it was a way of ensuring us that any other outcome was mathematically impossible. Zero percent chance could not be fixed. Healed. Or Reversed. Zero percent chance could not be turned into anything other than a zero percent chance?

But a different type of mathematics must have been taught to my wife in her south Louisiana schooling because she'd refused to accept the doctor's calculations. When given the same zero percent chance declaration, she'd dared to believe in something far more certain than any mathematical equation.

That cold December evening, while she was in that room clinging to hope, I sat in the hospital parking lot and prayed she was right. And I prayed she would be right quickly because we had just crossed the 24-hour mark and I knew time was not on our side. As certain as Christmas Day would arrive eight days later, it was also certain that our situation was going to have to be addressed soon. And the fact there was nothing I could do to control any of it made me want to go find that 6 pack and head West. Far away from all the unknowns.

CHAPTER ONE

Clean Sheets

September 2011

The vibe at our church felt more like a concert than the traditional, South Louisiana Catholic services Erin had spent her youth attending. Kind of like a Phish show, but with Jesus. As I stood there in my suit, wrinkled from the day's hard work of conference calls and meetings presenting insurance data that was slightly more exciting than audit results, I saw Erin dutifully waiting her turn in line. Her five-foot two-inch lean silhouette seamed to beam with the excitement of a kid waiting in line to enter Disney World for the first time. Her brown eyes glanced my way, and I caught her attention as she stepped onto the platform that would lead her into the baptism pool.

As I watched Erin's dunking, I was filled with love and confusion, which after five years of marriage, I had learned was a fairly consistent state of being. For many years Erin had fostered an intimate relationship with Jesus, but for some reason, on this night in early September, she was motivated to once again step into the baptismal pool. As she emerged from the water and headed toward me, I felt that love grow a bit more even as the confusion bubbled up and out of my mouth.

"You look so beautiful! Congratulations! But remind me why you wanted to be baptized? You did this in college. And you grew up Catholic, so I imagine you had that sprinkling thing when you were born, right?"

"Blake, you ask too many questions. What's wrong with me showing everyone that I love Jesus and have made Him Lord of my life?"

Finding it hard to formulate a proper rebuttal to that, I simply agreed. "It's just that I never thought of baptism as a rise and repeat kind of thing. But I do know that I love you, and I am so glad I was here to see this. Also, how cool is it that we will be able to tell our second born that they were baptized with you."

"That will be sweet, but I wonder if Rebekah will be jealous?"

"I would hope not," I responded. "I mean, I know you are getting yourself baptized more frequently than most, but since Rebekah was born just shy of two years ago that would seem to be a little quick. Even for you."

Erin punched me in the stomach as I laughed and hugged her soaking wet small frame. As we walked toward the ladies' room, Erin told me something that I had no way of knowing would impact our lives forever.

Pushing her wet black hair aside so she could focus her brown eyes directly on me she said, "As I was being baptized, I prayed and asked the Lord to not let this just be something I did, but to increase my faith and change my life forever."

Clean, crisp sheets. It's strange what you remember when you look back on pivotal moments in your life. Maybe this detail sticks out because after that night of post-baptism celebration we had fallen into a sleep so completely content and at peace. The smell and feel of those clean sheets added a last little luxury of perfection to our day. What I don't remember is when I first heard Erin crying out my name.

Jolted awake, I found myself alone in our bed. How many times had she called for me? It couldn't have been many because the wall that separated our headboard from the bathroom in our 1940's bungalow lacked enough insulation to make a small bed for a squirrel. Her urgent tone tugged my body toward her voice before my mind caught up. My emotions must have been in the same express lane as my body because they crashed into my mind before it was able to register a rational thought. Images of horrible bathroom scenes sprang to life as I sprinted toward Erin.

"I think we lost the baby." Erin's words slammed into my chest, smothering my breath.

Her desperate eyes drew words from a dry well inside me. "Are you sure?"

"There's a lot of blood."

Sinking to the cold tile, I gathered Erin's petite body close to mine, resting her head on my shoulder. As we embraced in shock, unable to quite comprehend how to feel, my mind stepped outside myself and gazed at us from overhead. The image of our huddle was surely similar to the countless couples who had agonized through this exact same moment in their own bathrooms. People I knew personally. An awareness of the lack of compassion I had shown them haunted my thoughts.

Erin's voice broke through the darkness, simply and beautifully. "Let's pray."

I wanted to pray, and I did pray, but I secretly wished I could borrow some of Erin's faith so I could really pray like I knew she wanted and needed me to. After our prayer, we remained fixed to the bathroom floor, as if we were a new accessory.

Time became irrelevant. A fresh and gentle bond enveloped us as we spoke in hushed tones, called the doctor's emergency line, and even laughed when I reminisced about the time she'd stopped up the tub with bubble bath on Valentines night, and I'd had to empty it with a bucket by throwing the gummy water out the tiny bathroom window while wearing only my birthday suit. As we talked I wondered if we were the only couple in our quiet little town sitting together, laughing through tears.

After our trip down memory lane, the conversation turned more profound and questioning. Not the type of questioning that asks why this happened, but rather why this happened on this particular night? Just hours after Erin had walked toward the Lord with such humility and joy. With such unshakeable faith. Why would the Lord allow this baby to enter heaven on this very night?

Erin turned her questioning into prayer. "Lord, You gave us this baby. You give and You take away. Either way, I will bless your name."

While my heart wanted to agree, it was fumbling toward this faith. Could I pray this prayer honestly even if our baby was…I couldn't find the courage to finish that thought.

Sometime before daylight, we returned to the clean sheets.

Their pristine whiteness seemed ironic now. Even though her heart was hurting, Erin's beautiful and complete trust in God ushered her quickly back to sleep. This rest-filled trust was as elusive to me as was sleep. I needed to channel the tornado of thoughts rampaging my mind. Instinctively rolling over, I opened the bedside dresser and pulled out my headlamp and well-used journal so I could process with full transparency my conflicting thoughts of this very private experience.

> It is about 2:45 a.m. and we think we could have lost our baby. I'm surprised at some of the emotions I'm feeling. My first instinct was pretty pathetic as I thought of the sympathy people would show us and how we would get to shine as examples of strength in the faith. I got to feel even worse after that when I realized I did not even have that kind of faith. I played out how our friends would care for us, and I wondered if I have truly cared for others the way we were going to need it now. The woman in our office who lost her mother recently, I have not even said anything to her about it even though I pass her desk every day. My friend tragically lost his son recently, and I have wanted to do something, but I have yet to do even the simple thing of writing him a card. I thought about sending my friend Justin in Montana an email telling him about this night just because I wanted to feel that human connection. I could really use a hug from a friend right now. What about Erin's dad? We haven't told him yet about the baby, and now this news might really

hurt him. I guess what sums up my feelings right now is this: There are so many people I know will care for us during this time...how inadequate has my friendship been to them? I know relationships are to be treasured and tended to...but I have allowed myself to think I'm too busy to check on people. Jesus, thank you for never being too busy for me. Especially right now.

CHAPTER TWO

Misdirection

My mind searched to find any other place to visit rather than imagining the scenario my truck was driving toward. Erin's OBGYN was still several minutes away, and my heart already hurt with the thoughts of seeing my wife's face in the waiting room. So I happily distracted myself with the sights of Homewood, the town we loved and the best place on earth to raise a family and build community. A small town nestled into the largest city in Alabama, Homewood sidewalks were busy every morning with parents walking their chattering kids to school, busy again every evening as families took their dogs on after-dinner strolls, and once a year, jam-packed with thousands as our Christmas parade proudly rivaled anything a larger city could offer. So many floats populated the parade it took more than an hour for them to wait their turn to leave the library parking lot, which conveniently for us, stood across the street from our house.

Homewood also housed The Trak Shak, a running boutique where Erin and I'd first met. As I passed the corner where the Trak Shak stood, my mind settled into a fond reverie, a much better place to visit on the drive to meet Erin.

May 2004

I'm a fairly organized guy. But for some reason I never remembered to put an extra pair of socks in my running bag. And after a while I guess I simply forgot them on purpose. Washing and folding socks was low on my priority list, so this had become a reasonable way to cut down on my bachelor duties. However, one pastime very high on my list was the Wednesday night running club at the Trak Shak.

This mid-week party started with a meeting of a couple dozen runners, followed by a three- to five-mile run, and ended with an after-party of beers and pizza. On one of these nights, I noticed an attractive woman with shiny brown straight hair flowing down toward her slender build, and I immediately strategized how I could coincidentally engineer an intersection of our paths. My moment happened as she left her friend to walk up and top off her beer. Great idea. I could use another one, too.

"Hey there, I'm Blake," I said in my best nonchalant voice, especially since she was much more attractive up close. "Is this your first time running with the group?"

"Nope," she answered, barely making eye contact.

"I've never seen you here before. What's your name?"

"Erin," she smiled. Good sign. At least we were smiling and making eye contact. "What's with the socks?"

Confused, I glanced down and remembered I'd forgotten my running socks again.

"You're wearing dress socks to run in," she said, grabbing her beer and glancing down at my white calves and black dress socks. Still smiling, she tossed her goodbye over her shoulder as she walked back to her friend. "See ya around, Sock."

Erin was very confident, which I liked; but very direct, which I definitely did not. Was she being cute or just rude? As I made my way back to my friends, I decided not to spend any time trying to figure it out. There was clearly no chance she would introduce herself as Mrs. Hamby one day.

Now, seven years later, turning into the parking lot at Erin's OBGYN, I chuckled out loud, thinking about how things had changed. Not only where we now married, but Erin had also carried that seemingly throwaway reference to me, Sock, and now used it in place of my name. As I darted through the rain and into the office, I longed to go back to those carefree days. Days when my biggest concern was looking silly in running clothes and black work socks. Days when Erin and I were just figuring each other out. Days when the last thing I would've imagined was meeting my wife at an appointment where we were bound to hear that we had miscarried our second child.

My eyes found Erin in the corner of the waiting room, legs curled up against her chest and arms wrapped securely around them. She looked as if she was desperately attempting to hold something inside. I guess in a way, she was. I gently kissed her on the head. Though her gaze stayed fixed out the window, the tiny streams of tears on her beautiful face ran like the raindrops on the window.

"How're you doing?" I asked, barely more than a whisper.

"Good…just…sad."

I searched for words that could rescue her from the sadness, but nothing came. Deep within me, there was a desire to be the hero my wife needed in the moment. But as we continued to talk, I realized Erin already had the Hero she needed.

"I was just sitting here praying," she said, a glint of hope in her eyes along with the worry. "I have to believe that if this is what the Lord has for us, then it is enough. He will take care of us."

Not only did Erin have the Hero she needed, she was probably closer to the hero I needed. I drew strength from her words, wondering how she could wrestle with such polar opposite emotions and yet possess the fortitude to choose faith over fear. Tears filled my eyes as I grappled with my own conflicting emotions. Thankfully I didn't have time to stew in my own feelings of inadequacy for very long before the nurse called our names. Erin grabbed my hand and led me back.

I'd been to the sonogram room during Erin's pregnancy with Rebekah, and during those visits I found the soft lighting a nice respite from the chaos of our busy lives. But during this visit the darkness seemed to outshine the light.

"So, you think something might have happened last night?" the porcelain-faced technician asked. She had kind eyes and wore on her collar a small golden pin of two baby feet.

Our silent nods and no further explanation revealed even kinder eyes, and I wondered how often she was the unfortunate messenger in situations like these.

As she gently rolled the sonogram handle over Erin's tummy, my breath had trouble making its way out of my mouth as anxious anticipation restricted my airways. I awaited the words that would state the inevitable. Words that would rip from us any hope of waking up from this nightmare to a better day ahead.

"There's definitely a baby in there," the tech stated. "Let's see what we can hear."

And just like that, the shwooshings of a baby's healthy heartbeat reverberated through the room. A broad smile spread across her face as she announced, "Your darling is alive and well!"

There was a pause before Erin broke into ugly crying. I stood staring in shock.

"You're sure?" I asked.

It was as if our minds would not allow our hearts to believe the good news. I wanted to exclaim, "So your telling me there's a chance!" like Dwight from Dumb and Dumber. But without all the childlike excitement. We questioned the poor technician again and again, and through our repeated interrogations, she graciously delivered a happy report. It felt like she was almost as excited as we were to not have to give the opposite report. After a few more tears, too many hugs, some awkward comments and Erin inviting the kind technician to come over for Thanksgiving dinner, a nurse escorted us to the obstetrician's office.

Waiting hand in hand, I felt so close to Erin. She had been the rock for both of us, but somehow she now transferred her strength to me, allowing me to feel like I had done my job as a husband.

With a height of almost six feet, Dr. Stephens entered the room, stoic and strong. Erin had been a patient of Dr. Stephens for several years and she respected her not only for her medical knowledge but also for her faith. They had walked together through some challenging situations, and for that Erin was grateful and trusting.

"Looks like things have started off a little tough this go around," Dr. Stephens said, clicking through a few screens on her laptop.

"That's one way to put it," Erin commented. "What do you think happened?"

"Some pregnancies just have more bleeding than others. But I don't remember you having this issue with Rebekah?"

"No," Erin said. "That was a very easy pregnancy."

"Good. And we're going to continue to pray that this one will be no different. But for right now, I would recommend you take it a little easier than normal, and let's get back together in a couple of weeks just to make sure things are good. If you have anything at all, come up before then, please do not hesitate to call."

Erin's face shone with relief as she gave me the "it's time to go" look, but I wasn't feeling it. What did the doctor mean that Erin could basically just go back to normal? Just a few hours ago, we were huddled on the tile of our bathroom, certain we'd miscarried.

"So," I said, halting Erin's exit, "What do we need to do when we get home? Like, specifically."

"You mean, tonight when you get home?"

"Yes. Tonight and tomorrow and the next day and for all the days after that until this baby gets here." I answered. "Specifically."

Dr. Stephens smiled. "Specifically. Go home tonight, cook dinner together, play with Rebekah, and then go to bed, as I imagine you didn't get much sleep last night. As for tomorrow, I would suggest doing the same thing. You can also follow that prescription for the day after that. Both of you can do whatever you normally do: work, go out on a date, exercise. Until—"

"Wait. You really think it's okay for Erin to work out? Go running? And what about her job at the school? She's teaching PE to elementary kids, and they—"

"Blake," Erin interjected, her voice steady, obviously trying to calm my nerves. "I think she knows what she's talking about."

Dr. Stephens leaned forward. "I understand last night was very difficult for the both of you. But I assure you, Blake, the baby has a very strong heartbeat, the bleeding has stopped, and we simply have to trust in God's plan. These peanuts are far more resilient than you can imagine." Realizing Dr. Stephens was not going to give me a specific twelve-point plan to ensure this trauma wouldn't happen again, I pretended to let it go.

Later that night, laying in a new set of clean sheets, I reflected on the emotional highs and lows of the previous twenty-four hours. Erin's baptism. Staring death in the face. Hearing the baby's heartbeat. Not getting the specific answers I craved. Nestling now with my wife in my arms. On the one hand, I felt deep peace. On the other, my soul was still shaking like there was an approaching train running down the tracks of our normal and peaceful life.

CHAPTER THREE

Unremembering

Balloons provided the perfect explosion of color inside The Battle House Hotel in Mobile, Alabama. The hotel is a classic Southern structure that has stood in place about as long as Alabama has been Alabama. Symbolizing the unrelenting spirit of the South, this space has seen destruction by fire, countless changes in management, and several complete renovations. These rooms have housed leaders and lushes, down and outers and up and comers, weary travelers, everyday Janes and Joes, and for a while in the late seventies and eighties during a period of abandonment, the homeless. Not to mention the many Mardi Gras celebrations that any true Southerner knows are better left unremembered.

About a month after our scare, Erin and I were enjoying the results of the latest restoration, all thanks to The Retirement Systems of Alabama who had restored this dilapidated cavern that for decades remained an empty tomb where rats went to die and turned it back into a crowned jewel of hospitality.

But Erin and I weren't alone. My entire family had escaped here to honor my mother's retirement from thirty-five years of working in the public school system. The surprise had gone off without a hitch. So well, in fact, I feared we might have lost Mom to a heart attack when she opened her hotel room door to a rainbow of balloons, posters, and cheering loved ones. After reviving Mom from the shock, we'd all partied deep into the night at the rooftop pool. Any trouble Erin and I might have encountered previously during this pregnancy seemed as distant as the rats that used to call this place home. I exhaled for the first time in weeks. Little did I know, my exhale wouldn't last long.

"Call Amanda!"

Those urgent words shot me from my blissful slumber.

"What? What's wrong? What happened? Did you fall down? Are you hurt?" The repetition was not helping my mind wake.

Erin's feeble voice answered from beside me. "I don't know. Just call your sister."

Her serious tone triggered my body to kick into high gear. Reaching over to flip on the bedside lamp, I could now see my ghostly pale wife grasping the sheet, curled into the fetal position, shivering uncontrollably. She looked like a picture of our unborn child, desperately trying to be ok, but forced to hang on to life by a rope that was being yanked from her hands. Ripping back the covers, the stark image darkened. Erin was lying in a pool of blood. Grabbing my phone, I glanced over at Rebekah's pack-n-play, grateful she was still deeply asleep.

Three minutes after I'd made the call, my sister Amanda strode into our hotel room, bringing with her the focus and calm good caregivers possess. Award-winning nurses, both she and her husband wear their humble authority in the same way I wear a sport coat to a business meeting. She'd even thought to bring Erin something to eat, which for some reason made me feel better.

Amanda assessed the situation in the amount of time it takes me to decide which blue shirt to wear to work, and then even-temperedly said, "Let's go ahead and call an ambulance."

"Ambulance?" I struggled to process. "Why do we need an ambulance? Ambulances are only for people that are sick, or been in an accident, or that are old. And how would they even know where we are? We aren't at our house. The baby's only sixteen weeks. It's going to be ok, right?" My questions continued to scramble through nonsensical strings, until Amanda steadied me and told me to find my phone.

"But I don't know their number... here in Mobile."

Her voice as calm as ever, Amanda said, "911."

"Right." I sighed and typed in those three digits for the first time in my life.

I had no idea what the address was for the hotel, but apparently the paramedics had a system to find us because within fifteen minutes they were wheeling a stretcher into our once peaceful room at The Battle House. The next thing I knew, my mom was watching Rebekah, miraculously still sleeping, while the paramedics whisked Erin and I into some hidden elevator I'd never noticed before.

"Sock," I barely heard Erin whisper. "I'm so tired. So, so tired...like I'm drifting off into heaven..."

I couldn't process the implications of her weak words. Or maybe I refused them. A world without Erin was not a world I wanted to consider. The only response I could muster was to tell her that was not a place she wanted to go.

When the squeaky doors opened, the paramedics dashed us through a kitchen and then into the vacant dining hall of the Trellis Room. This was a room I had eaten in with many clients and one I never thought I'd be striding through in the middle of the night with my wife on a stretcher, wrapped in a space suit thing that looked like it came out of the movie E.T.

Wheeling out the front door of The Battle House, the frigid wind slapped my cheeks much like the cold and turbulent reality that was storming through my soul. As my mind skidded on the sheer ice of despair, Erin reached out and laced her fingers into mine. I searched her eyes and surprisingly found no fear, rather another one of her piercing looks of hope. And not the blind hope that maybe things might all work out in some faraway distant place where people better than us lived easy lives. Instead, her gaze held a confident hope that said, "No matter the outcome, there is something better on the other side."

Then she said those familiar words: "Let's pray." With this call to action, I felt myself ripped by the nape of my neck from the frozen lake of despair and planted back into reality.

"Yes. Let's pray." Kneeling down in the ambulance, I held her close and formulated my thoughts, commanding my mind to shift from a posture of uncertainty to a stance of faith. I felt like a kid in Sunday school realizing that God needed to be real, not just a figure in a cute song about a short man named Zacchaeus, but an actual miracle-working God. The God He promises to be.

As the ambulance inched away from the valet stand, my

prayer of faith began. This was the first time I could remember praying into a personal situation where the outcome seemed so dire and uncertain. Truly a life-or-death situation. Surprisingly, I found each of my words were a brick of confidence building a foundation for me to stand upon, and my hope began to arise.

In the shadows of my mind, contrasting thoughts fought for my attention. *What if what you're praying for doesn't happen? Where will your faith be then?* But I could not afford to entertain those temptations. Too much was at stake, and I chose to focus on the words of faith coming out of my mouth. Surely those shadows would dissipate if I ignored them.

The Mobile emergency medical team efficiently checked us in and promptly wheeled us to the ultrasound room. The removal of Erin's space suit blanket brought relief, but the crisis was far from over. We still had to survive the impending results from the ultrasound. What was the likelihood of our baby surviving a second midnight hemorrhage? Slim, at best. Once again, Erin's soft hand snuggled into mine, almost as if placing her heart in the protective covering of my strength.

Seconds felt like hours as the technician prepared Erin's belly. The only sound I heard was the pressured thumping of my own heartbeat in my ears. Until...shwoosh, shwoosh, shwoosh.

"Looks like we have a strong heartbeat!"

While we were completely stunned, each swoosh covered us

with relief like lapping waves of the ocean.

"I don't understand." I confessed. "How is this possible?" As soon as I spoke, I regretted my words, afraid questioning would crumble the good news we had heard.

"All I can say is," the technician answered, "this heartbeat is proof you have a very real and very alive little baby."

Erin and I reveled in the steady pulse of our baby's beating heart.

"Mr. and Mrs. Hamby," a nurse broke the silence. "Your mom and sister are here. Can I send them back?"

Tiptoeing into our room, both my mom's and sister's faces lit up at the sound of the heartbeat.

"Beautiful," whispered my sister, Amanda.

After several moments the technician packed up, and my family couldn't contain our gushing emotions. Now we had two sonogram specialists invited to our house for Thanksgiving.

Left alone, the four of us attempted to process all that was happening. "How did our run-of-the-mill lives turn into an episode of Grey's Anatomy?" I squeezed Erin's fingers.

"Everyone's life seems run-of-the-mill"—my mom answered—"until it isn't. I'm sure the hundreds of people in this hospital feel the same way."

Digesting this profound thought, I vowed to notice more. To see those around me who have found themselves evicted from their normalcy and into a nightmare. I prayed God would help me to see what He sees, to not be so wrapped up in my own world that I failed to see the people hurting right around me.

Always aware of other people's needs, Amanda spoke softly. "We'll be out in the waiting room when y'all are ready to drive back to The Battle House."

Interrupting their exit, Erin remarked, "I don't know what the Lord is up to, but you mark my words, this baby is a miracle."

Everyone smiled at what seemed to be a cliche´ statement, responding with other Christian phrases equally cliche´. As my mom and sister left, a new doctor, fresh on the floor from the most recent shift change, brought even more cheer into our room.

"Y'all couldn't find anything better to do on a Friday night than come and visit us?" We instantly felt a connection to her spunk and vitality.

"Well, you know us Birmingham folk," I said. "Never a dull moment."

"Ha! Apparently not. And from looking at your charts, it seems that even though you're only in the beginning of your second trimester, y'all are trying to start a trend of late-night excitement with this little baby. But after reviewing your tests, I'm pleased to report that you have a very healthy, and very rambunctious human growing inside you."

I had to know more. "So, do you think this rambunctious

baby is causing these issues?"

"Oh no. Not at all." The doctor looked at both Erin and me. "Have you ever heard of a subcutaneous tear?"

"Oh, for sure. We studied that in biology class at my rural Alabama middle school."

The doctor scrunched her forehead. Erin smacked me in the arm. No one appreciated my attempt at levity.

"Sorry, Doc. We've never heard of it."

She smiled. "Well, that is what I believe we are dealing with. Sometimes a woman can experience a small tear during pregnancy, and that can cause additional bleeding. While it seems frightening, it's generally not something to get too worked up about. Erin, you simply need to take it a little easier than normal, and everything should be fine."

After a few more questions, Erin and I were once again alone. And also once again, we were relieved to learn everything was fine and that she just needed to lay low. But I still struggled to line up those statements with our reality. Two episodes of midnight hemorrhaging, this last one with my wife almost going into shock or worse, were not my definition of fine. I hated to admit it, but I might've been more comfortable with the doctor telling us that nothing was fine and everything might crash and burn. At least that would've made more sense.

Back at the hotel, I gathered with family around the breakfast buffet in the Trellis Room, chatting about how crazy it was that just a few hours earlier, paramedics had wheeled Erin out through a secret Batcave elevator. Erin stayed for a moment, but then wanted to go upstairs alone to shower and get some rest. I kissed her goodbye and told her to be careful. "Careful? I don't think there is a bear or wolf that is going to get me on my way to our room."

"Just try and take care of yourself," I said as I walked with Rebekah and my family toward the breakfast buffet.

After breakfast as my carefree Rebekah and I were playing in the large domed lobby of The Battle House, my phone rang. It was Erin, and when I heard her voice, I thought she might have encountered a bear on her way to her room. Her uncontrollable sobs triggered my breakfast to burn in my stomach and before I could muster words, my mind flashed images of Erin once again laying on the bathroom floor in a pool of blood.

"What is it?!" All I heard was more crying.

"Erin, what is wrong?" I sprinted toward the elevator, my mind not even aware I had just left my one-and-a-half-year-old precariously dancing up the stone stairs across the lobby.

"I...I..." Erin said between sobs. "I just finished my shower and was sitting on the stool brushing my hair and thanking the Lord for protecting us and the baby and...I...The...I heard the Lord say, 'This baby will be called Faith.'"

As if from a hidden camera at the top of the dome, I could see myself racing through the magnificent lobby, Rebekah on the other side crying because I'd left her alone, people turning their heads, and then I just stopped. Erin's words froze me, not by wonder or amazement, but by something altogether different. Aggravation.

"Okaaaay," was all I could muster. Pivoting on my heel to go rescue my daughter, my logical mind kicked in. "That's nice, Erin. But seriously, you just about gave me a heart attack. I thought the bleeding...I thought that something had happened again."

"No, nothing like that," she said happily. "I just wanted to share that with you."

Any further words, the ones I wanted to say anyway, would only lead to a fight, so I told her I loved her, that we'd be upstairs in a little while, and we hung up.

In that moment, Erin's message from the Lord meant about as much to me as the cantaloupe I had left uneaten on my breakfast plate. What I did not know at the time, what I had no possible way of knowing, was that those words spoken to Erin were very real and extremely powerful, a tangible force that would resonate across our life's path in ways I could never have imagined. All I could think about was how I longed to be like those Mardi Gras revelers and unremember the memory of Erin curled in a ball, shivering in a pool of blood in our hotel room.

CHAPTER FOUR
Turbulence

On a flight from Carrollton, Georgia to Lafayette, Louisiana, in November of 2010 was when my unnatural fear of flying started. Aboard his four-seater airplane, Wayne was the guy who always had everything under control, no matter the situation. Wayne and I had known each other for years, and he wasn't just my business partner, but my mentor and the owner and pilot for the flight that would carry him and I and another coworker to Louisiana. As we took off on that fall evening for a quick overnight business trip, I was tossing popcorn in my mouth and cutting up with my coworkers. That was until, somewhere over a nameless city in the Mississippi Delta, wrapped in the cover of night, the weather decided to join our party.

As the weather hit us with as much force as Serena Williams hits a tennis ball, Wayne didn't completely lose his cool, but his cavalier joking evaporated as quickly as my palms turned into an anxious sweaty ball. Plane rides are never supposed to feel like class five white water rafting adventures. Reaching for my Bible in my bag at my feet, I held it close to my chest. If we were going down, it was probably better to keep the Good Book close just in case that counted for something when St. Peter opened the pearly gates.

Once our wheels screeched to a halt in Lafayette, Louisiana, we were dazed as our rubbery legs stepped down the metal staircase to the runway. Thank God, we all exited that plane with our lives, but I also left with a heavy emotional bag. Maybe it was the trauma, maybe it was because I was now a father, but that flight flung me into years of experiencing extreme fear and panic whenever a flight got a little dicey.

Such was the case for the flight I was on a year later from Birmingham to Cleveland on a lonely November evening just a month after the scare in the hotel. While facing your fears and getting back on the horse is the right approach, my dread had not subsided over the twelve months since the first flight. In fact, this phobia had only seemed to intensify with each subsequent flight.

As the plane bounced around like a pinball being struck by random and powerful forces, I knew I had to divert my imagination from dying in an explosion of flames. Anchoring my thoughts in the present was not providing any relief. I tried to forget about the fact that in the last month we had twice found ourselves certain we had lost our baby. The weight of feeling there was nothing we could do but wait for the next disaster to happen seemed heavier than I was built to carry. I also tried to lose the pressure I felt because Erin's situation was not getting better but worse, or that she was continuing to experience bleeding, and for good measure now passing small clots. As these thoughts swirled through my mind in the same erratic way this plane was traveling through the air, I shut my eyes to search for a safe place to land. As I turned off the overhead light, I drifted toward another time. An earlier chapter in this ever-growing story of Erin and me.

May 2005

Anyone knows, summer temperatures and humidity in the South can soar. Most days just walking outside feels like you wrapped yourself in a warm, wet blanket. In this environment, working in the back of a U-Haul truck in the middle of May is basically a form a torture. And I was fairly certain I was going to strangle Bardwell.

Where is he?! He'd said he'd be here by 2:30 to help load this thing.

A drop of sweat splashed on my watch as I looked down to see it change from 4:01 to 4:02. On this Friday of Memorial Day weekend, the only thing that stood in my way of cool mountain air, a campfire, and a rafting trip down the Ocoee River was twenty more loads moved from my just-sold house and into the back of the U-Haul inferno. That and the time it would take to strangle Bardwell.

Echoing through the tin walls, the sound of a blaring radio crescendoed, and I peeked around the edge. Through the haze of heat, I spotted Bardwell speeding up in his shiny red convertible, top down. My frustration grew as I noticed he was dressed more for a beach trip than a moving trip.

"Dude, what happened to 2:30?" I didn't even look at him as I packed the mattress and started for the house.

"Oh, yeah, sorry about that. I went by Alabama Outdoors after work to buy this shirt. What do you think?" He posed. I was not impressed.

"I think you're an hour and a half late. It's hotter than Hades, and I am ready to go, so please grab a box and let's get this done." For the next hour, Bardwell loaded about two and a half boxes while I finished the rest. However, once we were on the road toward my storage space, each passing mile filled with sunshine and great music blew my aggravation out the open window.

My grandmother had a farm about an hour outside of Birmingham, and she graciously had offered to store my belongings. While her farmhouse lacked the vibrancy of its heyday, back when its eighteen acres flourished with crops that fed and paid my ancestors, the farm still resonated its beauty through its promise of a simpler time. As we turned right onto the dirt driveway toward her house, billows of dust clouds swelled behind us seeming to contain childhood memories—endless days of summertime exploring, cool nights sprinkled with fireflies, and the sounds of cicadas and locusts buzzing in the distance, lulling me to sleep.

It was 6:15 p.m. and I don't know if it was an act of redemption or simply the result of hunger, but Bardwell finally jumped in the game, and we unloaded the U-Haul in record speed. When we finished, we grabbed a Gatorade from the cooler and sat on the back of the tailgate, telling stories and laughing as the sun tucked itself in over the edge of the pasture.

"I'm so glad that's done," I said. "Now we can go to the campsite with nothing hanging over my head."

"Where're we gonna eat?" Bardwell groaned. "My stomach's so hungry it's eating itself."

"If my grandmother was here, she would have a great spread

for us, but she won't be here until next week. There's a bar in town that has great burgers."

"Let's do it."

"But we gotta get there soon or it'll get crazy. Think rowdy bikers. Wet T-shirt contests. Drin—"

"Wet T-shirt contests?" Bardwell had a gleam in his eye.

Laughing, I said, "Let's be gentlemen and just get to the campsite."

"Of course," he snickered sarcastically. "How many people we got coming to raft this weekend?"

"I think we have about eight. You know who I was really surprised said yes?" I asked. "That Erin girl. From the Trak Shak. Honestly, I didn't even realize I'd included her in the emails until she popped one right back and said she and another girl would be coming. Not sure I'm happy about that."

"Why?"

"I don't know. I hardly know her, but she's just so...I don't know. Aggravating."

"Ha! Sounds like love at first sight."

"No," I said emphatically. "Definitely not. She's cute, but she's also pretty direct. She just says whatever pops into her head."

Bardwell chuckled as he slid off the tailgate. "Let's get going."

Driving into the mountains toward the Ocoee River Basin in East Tennessee, my chest swelled with pride as I thought how free

I was. With the sale of my house, I had arrived at a place of no debt, a decent amount of money in the bank for a twenty-eight-year-old, and no other entanglements to speak of. I felt as free as Morgan Freeman walking on the beach in Zihuatanejo to meet his friend Andy Dufresne.

The next morning, as I sat just outside our tent door having my morning coffee, I thought I might have crawled into a portion of heaven: crisp mountain air and the sounds of a forest soothing my soul. The foothills of the Appalachian Mountains rolled before me like paint on God's canvas. This stretch had a long history of mining, and at one point loggers had stripped the vegetation through clear cutting. Thankfully those days were over, and my eyes scanned the horizon of evergreens repopulating and reclaiming their territory. The rapids in the distance called out like an invitation.

Bardwell and I had been relaxing in God's artwork for quite some time before the rest of the campers, including Erin, arrived mid-afternoon. With the goal of an introductory hike, we all worked together to set up everyone's camp so we wouldn't waste a moment of the sunlight.

Before we were even out of the campsite, I heard Erin remark, "Hey, Sock! What's with the backpack? Are you carrying that because you think it's cool?" As her words traveled across the warm afternoon air, I rolled my eyes at Bardwell. Classic bluntness. And that name, Sock... apparently she remembered my black running socks. I shot my answer over my shoulder, in similar fashion to her Trak Shak comment the year before at our first meeting that had apparently given me my new nickname. "Um, no. I think it carries my water bottles really well."

Catching up to me, she said, "You could just carry your bottle in your hand."

"Well, that is true. But then I'd have a harder time carrying the snacks I am bringing."

"Snacks? But we're only going on a two-mile hike. You don't need snacks." She chuckled.

"Maybe not, but I like to have them just in case. I also have some bug spray, mole skins in case of blisters, Neosporin, and other stuff like that, you know, just in case we might need it."

"Are you serious? We won't need any of that stuff; we'll only be gone about thirty minutes."

"Maybe," I said, trying to speed up the pace. If she got winded, perhaps she'd stop talking. "I hope you're right, but in the off-chance we do need or want any of that stuff, we'll have it with us. Besides, it's my back that's carrying it, so I'm curious why you care so much about what I am bringing?"

This was the first of what turned out to be many similar conversations between Erin and me. Me being overly practical, Erin living in the moment. Me making sure we're prepared, her simply flying by the seat of her pants believing everything was going to turn out okay. While this balance has suited us well as a married couple, it did not make for a peaceful hike.

Erin and I did not fall in love that weekend. In fact, when we were leaving, I was trying to get my friend Bardwell to ask her out. He was also from Louisiana, and I thought they might make a good pair.

However my time for falling completely and totally in love with Erin was coming sooner rather than later. Oh, and just for the record, about four miles into what turned out to be an eight-mile hike that day, Erin had eaten some of my snacks, had me carry her water bottle, and used not just my mole skin and Neosporin, but the bug spray, too.

The lurching of the plane jolted me from my mental escape and forced me back into the reality of where I was and where I was not. I was in Cleveland, and I was not with Erin.

Since the last few weeks had not provided a decrease in issues surrounding Erin's pregnancy, my sense of impending doom was steadily on the rise. Meanwhile Erin was as calm as ever, which led me to secretly question if she was losing her grip on reality. Yes, she believed God had spoken to her, telling her that this baby will be called Faith, but her physical body was not cooperating with that promise. Erin kept saying she was okay, but the bleeding communicated the opposite.

Standing by baggage claim, the revolving luggage represented my thoughts. Each suitcase, each concern bigger and heavier than the one before, coming by me so fast it was difficult to decipher which one I should let go by and which one to pick up and take with me. The last thing I felt up to was putting on a happy face and meeting my client for dinner to make small talk about nothing that seemed important. I wanted to be with Erin. As I tried to formulate a reasonable excuse to skip dinner and meet my client in the morning, my phone buzzed. I looked down, and my heart filled a little seeing it was Erin.

"Hey, how you doing?" I asked.

"Uh, Sock, I don't know." Her tone sucked out the hope that had tried to fill my heart, and I walked away from baggage claim.

"What's wrong?"

"I just feel really bad. I picked up Rebekah from dance and was heading home on the interstate and started to feel like I did that night in Mobile. My heart also started racing, so I thought it would be best to pull over."

"Wait. Are you on the side of the interstate?"

"That's where I was, and I didn't want to go any farther."

My heart now filled with sand, weighing down my body into

a chair. Families were all around me, greeting, laughing, and hugging. Anger burned at them for their privilege of closeness with their loved ones.

"Blake, it's cold and raining, and I can feel the wind blowing my car, and I'm afraid if I start driving again, I might get more anxious...maybe even pass out while driving."

"Okay, well, I think it's good that you pulled over, but I don't want you to stay there too long." The visuals pounded like hail in my mind. My distraught wife and young daughter parked on the shoulder of a busy interstate in the middle of a storm. The blood in the hotel. I sucked in a breath trying to stay calm. Erin did not need me projecting my fear onto her. What she needed was what she so often offered to me: Strength.

"Honey, we need to get you home. How about I call my mom to come and get you?"

"That doesn't make sense. What would I do with my car? Just hearing your voice makes me feel a little better. I wish I could make sense out of what I'm feeling."

"I wish I was with you."

"Me, too, Sock. But I think I might be able to drive again."

Knowing it was very unlikely I could convince her to sit there until my mom could drive to meet her, I suggested, "Why don't you take the next exit and use back roads to get to the house?"

Thankfully, Erin agreed.

"I'm going to call my mom to come over to our house to spend the night. I don't want you to be alone tonight. Something could happen, and you don't want it to be just you and Rebekah."

We prayed together, and Erin promised she'd call me as soon as she got home, and again when my mom arrived. With that we hung up.

In the middle of this busy airport with people buzzing all around, I felt like a man lost in the desert, desperate for any form of hope to come along and strengthen me. I staggered over to a wall of windows to hide my emotions. Anger surprised me with an urge to slam my fist into the glass. I realized I wasn't really angry at the fortunate people around me reuniting with their loved ones; I was angry at my life, this situation, the helplessness I felt, the fear that was bullying me. And right beside that anger was a shadow of guilt. My situation paled in comparison to so many others...nevertheless the anger burned. I imagined my fist shattering the window, shards flying every which way. A visual of how my life felt.

When my phone buzzed again, it was my client, and I did exactly what I did not want to do: answer it, put on my happy face, and confirm I would join them for dinner in about thirty minutes. Before I made my way back to baggage claim, I allowed the emotions to blow through me like the wind that had so violently rocked our flight. That anger melted into tears that streamed down my cheeks. Even though I was struggling to believe God had our best interest at heart, I asked Him to protect Erin and the baby and to carry me. In spite of myself, He apparently took pity on me as some level of peace floated into me through the shards of anger, fear, and questioning.

When I made it back to my hotel room after dinner, sleep was hard to find. I stared blankly at the wall where a picture of a boat hung. It was the exact same picture I had seen in so many other hotels of this chain. I wondered who took the picture. I wondered what their story was. Were they hurting right now also? Did they feel lost and alone? Did they know their picture hung on walls across the country? Did they feel like they were making a difference, or was it just something they did to earn a living? I thought about how pointless that picture was. It really wouldn't make much difference in how I slept that night. Rather like writing in my journal. If I wrote my thoughts down in a little black book, ultimately, would it make any difference to anyone or improve my situation?

But there was still this thing inside me that wanted to write my emotions down on paper. There had always been that desire in me. Why? I don't know, but it made me feel not so alone. So I did what I had done many times in my life, I turned to the page, and I let it all out.

> I am in Cleveland, Ohio. Came up here on a very bumpy flight and when I landed got a call from Erin and she was on the side of the interstate feeling bad again. I honestly hate this situation. I don't understand why these things keep happening to us. I know others go through so much more and when I think about that and how I am handling this, I feel even worse about myself. I wonder why I can't be as strong as they are.
>
> Why do I feel like I am falling apart under the relatively small weight of what we are carrying? Why am I so selfish? It's Erin who is experiencing the actual battles and physical pain and uncertainty, and she is the one who seems to be holding it together. Lord, what in the hell is wrong with me? I probably should not say hell to You. Sorry about that. Please don't make this any worse because I said that. Well, I am going to stop writing now and go back to staring at some cheap picture in my hotel room. Me and the person who took it are having a little telepathic thing going so I am going to try and follow that rabbit hole a bit more. Love you, Jesus.

CHAPTER FIVE

Shi!%y Situations

I n the weeks since my return from Cleveland, Erin continued to experience a steadily increasing level of bleeding and passing of clots. I was thankful she was able to get off the interstate that evening, but other than that, not much positive progress had found us. In fact, several days earlier, while on a dinner date, we'd found ourselves for the third time in an ER with large blood clots, terrible cramping, and sessions with ultrasound techs and doctors. How many times were we going to drive to the hospital only to be told everything was fine? Everything was not fine, as far as I was concerned. The apprehension for Erin and the baby weighed heavily on me daily, pressing as close to me as my shadow.

But that apprehension was not what I was going to focus on this night. This night I was on my way to a two year old birthday party for our close friends, Chris and Holly's oldest. Just about the time the sugar high from this evening had worn off our daughter, Erin and I were to drop Rebekah off with my parents and head to a fancy hotel for our anniversary. This was a trip I had been planning for months and one that was surely going to serve as a much-needed respite from the heaviness that was working so hard to keep my hope contained.

As I drove to the birthday party, I found myself alternating between thoughts of our anniversary trip and my most recent running experience. For some, running is an activity that should be reserved only for when something terrible is chasing you. I am not one of those people. Some of the most memorable moments of my life happened in the middle of a run. Like the time an owl attacked me. Or the time I ran so far, I got lost and had to hitchhike home. Or the time, just a couple nights ago, when nature called with no acceptable place to see a man about a horse.

My laughter from the mental replays of this incident broke the silence in my truck as I pulled up to the birthday party. Well on its way by now, I could barely wait to get inside and tell Chris about the epic tragedy that was my latest evening run. Tragedy plus time equals comedy, right? Forty-eight hours was enough for this debacle to be hilarious.

Chris's wife, Holly, greeted me at the door, took my coat and ushered me toward the huddle of adults standing around the food designated "hands off" from the kiddos. I slipped my arm around Erin's waist and hugged her, asking, "How are you feeling?"

"Let's just get through this party," she whispered into my ear. Searching her eyes, she smiled faintly and added, "I'm good."

I didn't believe her. But I needed levity and to be with people, so I chose to take her at her word, find Chris and dive into my story. Also an avid runner, he and I not only had finished several long trail races together, but also had met on many a morning to hit the pavement while darkness still hovered over Birmingham. If anyone would relate with my late-night excrement excitement, it was Chris.

"Did you catch the Heisman Trophy ceremony the other night?" Chris asked. "Yeah, but only after almost getting arrested," I laughed, and then launched into my sordid tale. Running in the bitter cold that night, I had traveled farther than I had planned when my nether regions began to wreak havoc. I needed a bathroom, and I "needed it now," so I sprinted, slightly hunched over, to the Homewood rec center which would be the last available restroom pitstop on my route...only it was already closed. My brain stumbled trying to remember where the nearest residential construction site would be; they always had a handy porta potty on site. Searching, I ran the best I could manage that night in my do-or-die situation. Chris laughed from his gut, making me do the same and forcing me to momentarily pause the story.

It felt so good to be doubled up like this. As a tear of laughter fell down my cheek, it dawned on me that I hadn't laughed freely for months. Just before getting to the climax of the story, my eyes met Erin's from across the room. Her grim expression was about as pleasant as the ending to my story. My laughter disappeared at the same time Erin disappeared into the guest bathroom.

"Wait. What happened next?!" Chris asked, still laughing.

"Hold on a sec..." I told Chris, as I made my way to the place where Erin disappeared.

Opening the door, I found Erin curled up in a ball on the checker-tiled floor. Her eyes were closed as she breathed slowly and purposefully.

"Sock. My stomach is cramping. I need to lay down here for a bit."

Kneeling down, I pulled her to my chest. She seemed so small and fragile, and it felt like an invisible cement boulder was weighing down and threatening to crush her. Protection burned from within me, anguishing to lift this burden from my precious wife. And yet simultaneously, I marveled at how incredibly tough she was. Ever since the night of her baptism and the false miscarriage, she had shown an uncommon faith, believing God's Word relentlessly in the face of every instance of extreme bleeding and every hospital visit. Maybe the cement boulder was crushing not on her, but me. Why are we here again? Why was her condition not getting better but increasingly worse?

Anxiety sucked my breath from my lungs and the walls of the bathroom closed in. Tunnel vision sparked the corners of my vision and roaring in my ears rose to engulf me. Panic. I had to get some air. Passing out next to my struggling wife in a powder room four feet from a child's birthday party was not a good option.

I steadied my voice. "Just relax. I'm going to get some water and be right back."

Stepping back into the party felt like I'd just taken a hit of something very strong and very illegal, as if I were in a scene from Fear and Loathing in Las Vegas. Everyone's faces and the chorus of "Happy Birthday" had become disfigured, like reflections from the mirrors of a carnival fun house. Chris's head was unnaturally pitched back laughing with a friend. Holly had an abnormally large knife, slicing into the birthday cake. Rebekah danced happy and carefree. Rebekah...How would her life change if her mother didn't come out of the bathroom alive? The last few weeks the bleeding had become worse. Clots so large I was not sure the baby had not come out hidden behind one. Could Erin be dying?

Bleeding from the inside out?

No! Stop it, Blake. You can't allow your mind to go there.

Exit was the only command my brain would respond to, and I snuck past the small crowd and burst into the freedom of winter air. My breath swirled in the frigid breeze, and for a few moments, I got lost in its wispy curls. Breathe in. Breathe out. Breathe in. Breathe out. Each shot of icy air into my lungs centered my mind until the panic retreated. Only then could I begin to act.

Back inside, I found Erin in the same fetal position on the tile floor of the restroom.

"Are you feeling any better?" I asked, already knowing the answer.

"I don't know."

Kneeling next to her again, I prayed. Not one of those prayers where you recite by rote what you always say because you know it sounds good, but rather the kind of prayer that rises from the depths of your soul. As the simple words flowed, the atmosphere changed. It felt like warmth rolling over us after being out on a cold winter day.

"God, I am asking you right now to heal my wife, to bring her out of this place of pain. To bring beauty from ashes, just like You promise in Your Word. I lift this baby up to You right now and proclaim that she will live and not die. Psalms 139 says You are knitting this child together in Erin's womb, and Your ways are perfect." The faith I had so often seen in Erin rose in me, cutting a pathway through the raging sea I had been living in. "God, nothing is impossible with You, and I am asking You to do the impossible. Right now. In Jesus' Name, Amen."

Erin lifted her eyes to mine with a look that said, I hope you know what to do. In fact, I need you to know what to do. I felt the weight of her needing me in ways that we had never explored before. In that moment, I thought about all the great explorers I had read about late into the night tucked safely into my bed. Men like Ernest Shackleford and John Wesley Powell. I wondered how they felt as they stared into the eyes of the desperate and frightened men on their team. Eyes that no doubt called out for confident direction in just the same way Erin's were calling out to me.

Mustering every bit of inspiration I could from my prayer, I nodded at Erin and said, "This is what we are going to do. I'm going to go out there, check on Rebekah and get her squared away, and then you and I are going to the hospital." When Erin simply acquiesced, not only did I know my instincts were correct, but also that we needed to act quickly. Erin is not the type to agree without a proper discussion of all the alternatives. She needed a doctor.

Holly was waiting for me outside the bathroom door. "What's happening?" she asked. "How is Erin? What can I do?" What a friend to be so in tune with our situation.

Within minutes, I'd hugged Rebekah goodbye, assured her all was well, and arranged for Chris and Holly to take care of her for the night. Then I carried Erin out to the car.

Driving toward the hospital, I checked on Erin as she scrunched herself up in the passenger's seat. She was in serious pain. The closer we traveled to the emergency room, the farther away the warmth of my prayer felt.

Hurling through the dark, chilly night, I prayed again. This time it felt more like a plea than a prayer. "Dear Lord Jesus, please do not take my wife from me."

CHAPTER SIX

Familiar Things That Are Unfamiliar

The ultrasound process started comfortably, like a new conversation with an old friend. We'd been here before, more times than we wanted. As the technician bustled around preparing both the machine and Erin's belly, the dialogue between us had an immediate familiarity. Until it didn't.

The ultrasound tech's body language turned stiff and controlled. Her lack of comforting words spoke volumes as she did her job with razor-sharp focus. And when she announced the sound of the baby's heartbeat, her phrases were absent of the calm excitement that had exuded from the previous ultrasound techs we'd met. I tried to excuse this by telling myself she had been absent the day they taught bedside etiquette. However, when we pressed for more information her only response before she left was a compassionate look and the words, "The doctor will be in soon to give you the updates."

Alone in the dimly lit room, the only hum was the ultrasound machine. How could that tiny hum feel louder than the screaming toddlers we'd just left at the birthday party? I attempted to crack a joke about how this was a nice start to our anniversary trip, to which Erin only mustered up a cordial smile.

A few minutes later, the lead nurse joined us.

"Good evening, I'm Jamie. How are you feelin', honey?" she asked Erin.

"I've felt better," was her only response.

"Are you still experiencing the cramping?"

"Yes."

"The readings we've received show you are contracting, so what we're--"

"Wait," Erin interrupted. "I'm contracting? How does that work? I'm only at twenty-two weeks. Are you sure?"

"Yes, honey, we are sure."

"Umm...I think we should take another reading to see if maybe there was a mistake," Erin insisted.

"I understand, and that is a very good suggestion, but we've already taken several."

"How? How have you taken several? I haven't been hooked up long enough for that."

"Sweetheart," Jamie placed her hand on Erin's. "You are contracting every minute."

That comment broke me.

Erin shook her head. "No. No. We need to make that stop. How do we make that stop?"

"Yes, we agree we need to try and stop the contractions, so we've ordered you a magnesium drip. The IV nurse will be here in just a moment to set that up." Jamie sat in a chair so she could face both Erin and me. Her tone became measured. "I need to talk to you about the information we received from the ultrasound that will explain why you are contracting. You have an abruption of the placenta."

"Abruption," I said. "What does that mean?"

"It means Erin's placenta has pulled away from the wall of her uterus."

I grasped for meaning. "Can we fix it? Can we sew it back into place?"

"No, it unfortunately does not work that way. When a placenta detaches, it basically stops the flow of all the nutrients that are needed for the child. It can also cause heavy bleeding for the mom, which we do not want. What we are seeing is that your placenta appears to be roughly 50% separated. With the contractions happening every minute, we want to watch you very closely. So we are going to admit you."

"Wait a minute," Erin stated. "You can't admit me. Tomorrow is the last day of school before Christmas break, and I have to be there. I need to go to work tomorrow."

"Honey, listen to me," Jamie tried to find the right words. "You can't go home tonight. In fact, you will be in this hospital until the baby comes."

"What?!" Erin was riled, and I reached out to hopefully calm her down. Excitement was certainly not going to help stop the contractions. She jerked away from my touch. "Miss Jamie, I am not going to live in the hospital for the next four months! I can't do that. I'm only at twenty-two weeks. I have a daughter, and a job..." Erin was trying to comprehend how all of that could possibly work.

"Erin, look at me," Jamie said softly. "I am so very sorry to say this, but you will be lucky if this baby makes it another twenty-four hours."

Silence.

Then Erin melted into uncontrollable sobs.

CHAPTER SEVEN

Mountains

The haze of the next few hours was saturated with tests, questions, various medical professionals, more tests, and more questions. I sought every face for some hope and asked my own questions to hear solutions. But good news was nowhere to be found. Between visits from doctors, I called my parents and they immediately drove the hour to be with us. The presence of my family more than made up for the lack of comfort from the medical community. My sister and our good friend, Brian Tanner rallied beside us as well. My gratefulness to not have to carry this alone was immeasurable.

Well after midnight, the nurses started a magnesium drip in an attempt to stop Erin's contractions. As the medication coursed into Erin's veins, it looked as if hope was also pouring through the tiny needle. I watched as Erin seemed to arise from beneath the weight of questions to stand once again. Amazed at her ability to recover emotionally so quickly from the shock that she would not leave until the baby came, I remembered her anchor. She was sure that God had promised her this baby would be called Faith...as sure as the sun would rise in the morning. While I was also sure of the sun, my focus seemed to be fastened not on its rising but its setting. And the darkness that inevitably follows.

As the last nurse left, she kindly suggested we both try to rest. When the door closed behind her, I longed to be on the other side of it. The side that did not contain the anguish of our present reality. The side where my wife's and my unborn child's lives were not hanging in the balance. Sighing deeply, I realized I was still in my suit pants and standard blue button-down shirt. The setting for that attire seemed as far away and impossible to get to as the moon.

"How are you feeling about that anniversary trip for tomorrow?" I asked, trying to bring some humor into the room.

"The bed at Ritz-Carlton Reynolds Plantation would be more comfortable than this one, I'm sure."

"Good point." I tried to chuckle. "Speaking of, how is that bed? You got room in there for two?"

Erin smiled. "I think I could make some room for the right person. But you just try to keep your hands to yourself. We don't want things getting out of control. We might end up pregnant."

"Who needs Reynolds, anyway, and all their fancy candlelit rooms? These monitor screens create all the romance we need."

After our verbal dance, I untied my shoes, placed them neatly under the bed, and curled beside Erin. In a matter of moments, I felt her body twitching to sleep, and I knew the mood lighting would not prompt any more romantic dialog this night. No more jokes to distract me from my own mind. With the jokes gone, those thoughts lurking in the dark shadows of my mind crawled out and filled the emptiness of the room.

As those thoughts slithered to life, they took shape before my eyes and appeared as an immovable obstacle materialized directly in my path. The more this vision crystalized, the more it seemed an actual mountain towered at the end of our hospital bed, a Mt. Everest rising out of the flatlands of the hospital floor. Towering, menacing, dominating, it taunted me to try to climb it.

Gazing upon this towering enemy, I again recalled the many adventure books I had read about how men and women throughout centuries had traveled to mountains like these to test themselves. To discover if they were worthy. To experience what it takes to conquer the mountain. To forge on when the path forward disappeared. When only unknown territory lay ahead.

Experiencing those pages in the safety of my bed, I had often wondered if I would have the courage it took to be one of those adventurers, to stand at the edge of uncertainty and, instead of being repelled by it, be drawn into it? Laying there in that hospital bed, I found my answer: No. A resounding no. This mountain represented a twenty-two-week-old child that was hanging on by a thread inside my wife, and I did not have what it took to believe that my baby could hang on another four months. I felt the oppression of this mountain with all its jagged peaks and cold dark crevices and realized it also represented the reality that my wife could very well be bleeding internally and possibly slip away as well, and there was nothing I could do about it.

The roar of my heartbeat charged down the mountain like an avalanche, warning me to stay away as despair engulfed me.

But somewhere in the chaos, a whispered thought snuck in. "If you have faith the size of a mustard seed, you can command this mountain to go. And it will." I searched for these seeds of faith in my heart and found none remaining.

But yet another whisper met me inside the chaos. "When there are two or more gathered in My name, I will also be gathered with them." Then another. "One can put one thousand to flight, but two can put ten thousand to flight." While the avalanche of despair continued to bury me, these thoughts crept in to hold me just enough as to not be completely overcome.

My mind raced. Who in the world did I know that was crazy enough to join me on this adventure? Who would stand at the base of this mountain and have the faith that God could do what His Word said? Who has so much faith spilling over that I could drink in the overflow? Faith that even if the worst happened, he would still charge forward? Who could come into this avalanche and rescue me?

The corners of my mouth curled into a smile. Matthew Calhoun, that's who.

Just thinking about having Matthew come and pray with us strengthened my faith. Matthew is not the type of friend who will get you from jail early on a Sunday morning. He is the type who will sit next to you in the cell. He is also the friend who would walk out of the jail with you straight to church and raise his hands in surrender and worship to a God he knows heals him, forgives him, and makes him brand new. Knowing I had someone who could spread some faith in our situation built up a fresh confidence inside me. I felt as if I was already being pulled, slowly, from the depth of the avalanche.

And with those tiny whispers, I knew exactly what I needed to do to start the journey over this mountain: I simply needed to take a step forward. I needed to move even if I was unsure about the route. Even if I was unsure we could even survive. Even if there was no chance of safety. I just needed to move.

The new hope flooded images of others who willingly stepped into their own great unknown. John Wesley Powell, the one-armed Civil War general standing on the banks of the mighty Colorado, preparing to push into his great unknown. Sir Edmund Hillary and Tenzing Norgay, daring the Death Zone of Everest, knowing that every step they took forward was a step away from safety but also toward an uncertain glory. Rosa Parks, who courageously stepped onto a bus with uncertainty and fear but also propelled by immense hope for a better day. Erin's and my situation was so different from each of these brave souls. But despite those differences, I found strength in knowing that they too looked upon their mountains and summoned that mustard seed of courage and faith to take a first step. And then another. Maybe the time I had invested, tucked safely into my warm bed, reading their stories had served a purpose. Maybe God had given them to me for such a time as this.

Laying there in the hospital bed, my arm around Erin, the strength that comes from standing on the shoulders of giants compelled me to speak. It was less of a prayer and more of a conversation with God about my fears, my concerns, my inadequacies. The more I spoke, the more my words turned to the truths that settled my feet on the edges of that mountain. My feet started to feel like they'd found something firm. I don't know how long I laid there talking out loud to God, but it was long enough to find that same deep and contented sleep that Erin had so quickly found.

CHAPTER EIGHT
Zero Percent Chance

Morning crashes early when you're in the hospital. "Sorry!" said the nurse. "We didn't mean to wake you."

Then don't make so much noise, I didn't say out loud.

"How are you feeling?" Dr. Stephens's familiar voice brought Erin and me to an alert state. We both wanted to hear what she had to say about our situation.

"I feel like I just lost a boxing match," Erin said through a smile.

"That sounds about right."

I could tell Dr. Stephens was attempting to approach us with the same casual small talk that normally accompanied Erin's visits, but she could not find the cadence. The gravity of the room would not allow it.

Putting on gloves and pulling up a rolling chair to the end of the bed, the doctor said, "Erin, I need to check you. Please bear with me for a moment."

Barely awake and hobbling to find my footing outside the bed, I watched as the doctor placed her hand inside my wife to check her cervix. Several seconds later, my mouth dropped in shock as she brought out a handful of clotted blood, the size of a large apple. With only eye contact, the doctor directed the nurse to bring over a trash can. After disposing of the clots, she checked Erin again. Another handful of clots. Chills shot through my body as my eyes gaped at the sight. Dread swallowed my gut.

Erin was oblivious as she chirped at the nurse. "How are you doing today?"

"Good," the nurse said with concern in her voice. "I'm good."

"What's your name?"

"Pam. I'm Pam."

How could Erin's and my experience at that moment be so drastically different? I wanted to throw up, and she was chatting casually with the nurse?

Dr. Stephens rolled off the gloves, asked the nurse to draw blood, then walked over to Erin and gently touched her hand. As she looked down at Erin, I could sense her mind was reeling with information she didn't want to communicate. Or was that me? I wasn't sure.

"You look good, honey, and you're holding up well. The good news is the contractions have stopped."

"That's great!" Erin exclaimed and smiled at me. I was frozen and could not share in what she thought was a victory. And neither did Dr. Stephens.

"Pam is going to take a blood sample, and I'll be back shortly and see how things are going."

Before Dr. Stephens left, Erin squeezed her hand, looked her in the eye and said, "I am so glad you are here. Knowing you're the one looking over us makes me feel so much safer."

A small thank you was all that Dr. Stephens said before she turned and walked out of the room. I think she couldn't stay for fear of Erin reading the conclusions on her face, the understanding that her experience and education could foretell where this was heading.

Nurse Pam's freckled countenance was both confident and inviting, like we were just about ready to sit down to a large homemade meal at our Mom's house. I guess in some ways Erin took comfort in knowing that Erin's Mom's name was Pam also.

Whatever the reason, I was thankful Pam was the nurse assigned to our room.

"Erin, I'm going to draw some blood, but I'm really good at it so you'll hardly feel a thing."

"I'm so glad Dr. Stephens said the contractions stopped. Thank you, Lord!"

"Good news, yes, but we also need to make sure we are focusing on you. It's important for you to be okay, along with the baby."

"I feel much better than last night."

"I know you do, but a placenta abruption is nothing to play around with, especially one that could be over 50% torn. You just keep trying to relax until the blood work comes back."

Once Pam left, Erin leaned back and closed her eyes. I wanted to close my eyes also and drift into a peaceful nap where all this reality did not exist, but sleep was not an option. Sitting there, I wondered, what does one do in a hospital room other than think about how bad things might be while waiting for test results? I remembered our pastor talking about how the Bible says that God inhabits the praise of His people. That sounded like something I could use, so I grabbed my iPhone.

Nestling into the couch, I hit play on one of our favorite songs, "God is Able." After a forty-second guitar riff, the Hillsong team sang, "God is able, He will never fail. He is almighty God. Greater than all we see, greater than all we ask, He has done great things."

In the same way those familiar lyrics filled the hospital room, my heart also soaked them up like a sponge. The message warmed me—like a warm bath after being stuck in an avalanche. By the end of that short song, Erin and I tearfully looked at each other with hope in our hearts. In the warmth of the moment, Erin opened her YouVersion Bible app and declared Psalm 91 over our situation.

> *Whoever dwells in the shelter of the Most High will rest in the shadow of the Almighty. I will say of the Lord, "He is my refuge and my fortress, my God, in whom I trust." Surely he will save you from the fowler's snare and from the deadly pestilence. He will cover you with his feathers, and under his wings you will find refuge; his faithfulness will be your shield and rampart. You will not fear the terror of night, nor the arrow that flies by day, nor the pestilence that stalks in the darkness, nor the plague that destroys at midday. A thousand may fall at your side, ten thousand at your right hand, but it will not come near you. You will only observe with your eyes and see the punishment of the wicked.*

If you say, "The Lord is my refuge" and you make the Most High your dwelling, no harm will overtake you, no disaster will come near your tent. For he will command his angels concerning you to guard you in all your ways; they will lift you up in their hands, so that you will not strike your foot against a stone. You will tread on the lion and the cobra; you will trample the great lion and the serpent.

"Because he loves me," says the Lord, "I will rescue him; I will protect him, for he acknowledges my name. He will call on me, and I will answer him; I will be with him in trouble, I will deliver him and honor him. With long life I will satisfy him and show him my salvation."

About 8:30 am, Dr. Stephens and Pam returned. We were happy to see them, but I sensed that the reluctance of Dr. Stephens could fill a wheelbarrow. She sat on the edge of the narrow hospital bed, placed her hand on Erin's leg and looked pointedly into her eyes. "How are you feeling?"

"So much better since Blake and I had some time to worship and pray together. I know the Lord is doing something great in this situation."

"Good." Dr. Stephen's eyes squeezed with the kind of smile your mom gives you right before offloading terrible news. Erin didn't seem to notice. "Since our last visit, I've looked over your chart some more and consulted with my partners, as well as colleagues in the high risk OBGYN practice. We've discussed the details, and Erin, I need you to know that everyone has come to the same conclusion that I do."

Here it comes. I braced myself and glanced over at my wife to see how she was doing. She was still floating well above reality in her own personal hope balloon.

"Erin, I believe," Dr. Stephens said carefully, "we all believe that we need to go to the next step and induce labor."

Erin's brow furrowed. "But I thought you said at twenty-two weeks the baby would not make it."

"There is a slight chance it could make it," she answered, "but generally, yes, there is a very low likelihood that it would survive."

Erin shook her head. "No. We don't want to do that. Blake and I don't want to push to have the baby. Everything we've been doing is to keep the baby in."

"I understand, but you need to know that this baby is going to come soon. Very soon, and it would be better to get the baby out."

"Why? I'm feeling better. The bleeding and pain have been happening for months; this time was just a little worse."

"Erin," Dr. Stephens scooted a bit closer toward her. "This time it was more than a little worse. A placenta abruption is not to be taken lightly. I know this is so hard to hear, but I truly believe this is the right direction for everyone."

"It is not the right direction for my baby," Erin said more sternly than normal.

Dr. Stephens did not have words to respond to that comment.

"I just don't understand, Dr. Stephens. We all know if we give birth now, our baby will not live."

Dr. Stephens's eyes again met with Erin's. "I know this is hard, Erin. Trust me, my heart is breaking with you. It's breaking for this baby. But the fact is, we need to get this baby out."

"But why Dr. Stephens? This just does not make sense. Tell me why you are saying this." Erin's eyes pleaded with mine to do something. I had to do something.

"Dr. Stephens," I said. "What are you not telling us?"

Struggling to find the right words, she finally released the news she'd been trying to avoid. "Erin, we have to take this baby. I don't think you understand how serious this is and how much blood you have already lost, that you are continuing to lose. If we are not careful, you could bleed out. I've seen it happen. No. We simply cannot save both you and your baby...and I have to save you. You have a young daughter already, and a husband, and they both need you here."

These words shot through my soul like a cannon blast, giving flesh to the lurking fears that had been harassing my mind. I was right. My wife's life had been hanging in the balance alongside the life of our unborn child. All the hope and peace I had so recently received poured out onto the floor through the cannon-sized hole in my heart.

Erin, on the other hand, seemed to be unmoved by this direct hit. She turned her face toward the window, wordless. But I knew she would not stay silent long. The motherly instinct to protect her child was too strong; Erin would be unwilling to allow her child to be put in a situation of almost certain death.

"Dr. Stephens," Erin implored, "I love you and I respect you. But I feel much better. And the contractions have stopped. I believe God is doing something here and I do not want to stop that."

The doctor's face grew tight. "Erin, this baby has a zero percent chance of survival. Zero. We need to turn our attention on you and ensure that your body can heal."

Zero percent chance. Wrapping my mind around these words was like attempting to grab hold of water I was drowning in while the shackle of despair pulled me under. Not only was our baby going to die, but our doctor had just confirmed the imminent danger of losing my wife as well. If Erin had a primal sense to protect her child, I shared a similar ferocious sense to protect my wife.

I leaned forward in my chair to reach out to Erin's hand and tell her we needed to trust Dr. Stephens. But as my mouth opened, Erin's words filled the room first.

"Dr. Stephens," she said with quiet boldness, "we believe in miracles. I am asking you to believe in miracles, too."

I froze. Erin's voice was soft, but the power of her fierce words pushed me back, forced me to stand down and sink back into my chair. Miracles. Could I believe in that? Hadn't we just prayed and declared our trust in the Lord?

Dr. Stephens felt it, too, because she also retreated from her stance.

Heavy silence engulfed the three of us as we separately dealt with our emotions.

Many seconds passed, or maybe it was hours. We seemed to be caught in a timeless vortex.

Meekly, from the corner of the room, Pam spoke. I had forgotten she was there. I think we all had.

"Dr. Stephens," Pam was focused on a computer screen. "Erin's blood work has just come back, and her hematocrit is at twenty-six."

Even though I was completely oblivious to what a hematocrit

was, I could tell from Dr. Stevens's reaction that this was important information. But she seemed puzzled by the number.

"Are you sure?" she asked as she went to read the results for herself.

"What does that mean?" inquired Erin.

"Hematocrit is your blood count. In your case it can give us an idea of the degree of internal bleeding your placenta abruption might be causing," Pam explained. "A normal range for you should be thirty-six to forty-six, so yours definitely is low."

"But it's not as low as I was sure it would be," Dr. Stephens added, but more to herself than to us. "This doesn't make sense." She stared blankly past the screen in deep contemplation. Was she rehearsing the amount of blood she'd removed earlier from Erin? Perhaps reviewing the conversations about our case she'd had with her colleagues? Maybe reliving the horrors of past experiences where a placenta abruption turned fatal? "Twenty-six," she whispered again.

When she gazed back over at Erin, still thinking, I was certain she was processing her thirty years of medical knowledge and balancing that with the conversation she'd just had as Erin professed her faith in what God could do.

"Okay," she announced with finality. "We will continue to monitor this closely for a couple hours and see what happens."

With that she stood up and left the room.

CHAPTER NINE

Birthdays

Hospital life. It's like a long drive through Kansas during tornado season: long patches of nothingness, all the while the threat lurks that at any second a spontaneous tornado could touch down, whip you into chaos and catapult you recklessly to certain doom. It's just enough boredom to lull you to sleep, combined with just enough anxiety to keep you from finding rest.

In spite of that, Pam's help was a gift, and she had been specifically assigned to take care of only us. I found that to be a lovely perk until I realized the reason. We had individual care because our situation was dire enough to warrant it. Either way, we were glad to have her with us because she had a knack for making us feel comfortable and at peace. And her jokes staved off my nervous boredom for at least a few minutes before my feet were once again itching to take me away from this room.

The moment Erin closed her eyes for a nap, I escaped the pressure cooker and paced through the maze of corridors. An aquarium wall here. Random artwork hanging there. Nurses' station after nurses' station. Laughter spilled from around the corner and the sound drew me like an oasis. A small boy was celebrating his birthday in the hospital gathering area, with balloons and family all around.

I had to sit in the presence of this joy; my soul craved the energy. Picking a chair in the corner so as not to appear a stalker, I closed my eyes and listened to his laughter as he tore open gifts with ease despite his IV. Sheer delight at a Lego set. Squeals at a remote-control car. I learned two wonderful things listening in. One, his surgery to remove his kidney had been a success, and the hope was he would live a long, healthy life. Two, the grandma with the birthday crown shared his birthday. As the family sang to both the boy and the older woman, I smiled. Shared birthdays. Erin and I also shared the same birthday, three years apart. And then I laughed out loud, remembering the birthday that nearly shattered any chance we'd ever share anything together again.

July 2006

California Interstate 5 stretched out before us like a scene of Forrest Gump running across America. As we exited the Sacramento Valley and entered the Cascade Mountain Range, Mt. Shasta overtook the entirety of our windshield. The magnificent sight dwarfed everything around us. Everything, that is, except the gulf between Erin and me as we sat two feet from each other. Maybe it was the stress of planning a wedding just a few months away. Maybe it was the realization we had been fighting more than usual. Maybe it was because we were internally avoiding our own doubts about the feasibility of our relationship. No matter the reason, the expanse between us seemed to expand with the same speed as Shasta neared.

Northern California was home to the JH Ranch, a youth leadership camp where we had served for two weeks as adult leaders with several other twenty-somethings. I would return home the next evening to Birmingham while Erin planned to stay an extra week for a special father/daughter event. This last night together should've been special but instead was a tight ball of tension. We had just dropped a camper off at the Sacramento airport and were driving back to the Ranch. All things considered, it would have been better for only one of us to have made the trip. In an effort to pull us together, I drove to a nice restaurant on the banks of Shasta Lake, one of the most gorgeously blue lakes I'd ever seen. As we nibbled on our food, I marveled that the magic of this spectacular scenery was unable to sprinkle any of its magic dust over our moods.

Later as the sun warmed everything but our hearts, we walked along the pier, and I felt the need to lighten the mood, to bridge the gap between us. Looking deeply into Erin's eyes, my arms reached out to embrace her, and for reasons still unclear to me, I did not stop at just a hug. Sweeping her into my arms, I impulsively strode to the edge of the pier and still clinging to my fiancée, plunged us both into the frigid waters of Shasta Lake.

As the cold water submerged us, Erin's arms pushed against my chest. I held on for just a second longer before releasing her. "How fun and spontaneous am I?" I thought as my head popped up above the surface. This is just what the doctor ordered. Until I saw Erin scrambling out of the water. Laughing, I continued to swim, hoping she would accept my invitation to play some more. Only instead of playing, she was briskly stalking up the pier toward the car.

"Hey! Why are you leaving?" I called after her. "Okay, maybe that was a bad idea. I just thought we needed to lighten the mood. Come on back!"

No response. Just more of the stalking. Time to get out of the water. Right now. And catch up. Running to her, I stretched my hand to gently grab her arm, and she recoiled from my touch like my hand was a red-hot poker. Anger and fear spread across her face. Now I was thoroughly confused.

"Erin," I said softly, "what in the world is going on? Why are you so mad?"

"Who are you?" she answered. "I cannot trust you!"

"What are you talking about?"

"You just tried to drown me!"

I stopped in my tracks. "What?"

When she spun to face me again, I said, "Hold on. Are you serious? What in the world would make you think that? I mean, we are engaged. I would never try to drown you. I'm a good person…I recycle, I don't smoke, and I mostly eat organic."

She was not amused.

Both of us fully clothed and soaking wet, we just stared at each other. And then we realized other people were also staring. Thankfully, their puzzled expressions ushered in a bit of humor. While Erin didn't pardon me fully for my alleged attempt to kill her, she did smile a little and was willing to get into the car with me. I counted that as a win.

Before we started back to the ranch, I removed my soaked shirt, and instead clothed myself in humor. Laughter had always been my go-to defense mechanism to diffuse tension. So I poured bad joke upon bad joke upon the already bad joke of trying to drown Erin in the lake. About an hour from the ranch, Erin sported a Cheshire grin. Two could play this game. Very calmly and casually, she removed her chewing gum from her mouth, looked at it, and smashed it squarely into my very hairy chest.

I took this as an olive branch. A creative way to get revenge for the lake episode. Sensing an opportunity to remove the distance between us, I tore the gum from my chest, looked at it, and squished it squarely into her hair, finishing it off with a good twist.

The next act in our little play sprang up in less time than it takes for the light to come on after flipping the switch. Erin contorted from a place deep down inside that we don't talk about in church and unleashed the worst barrage of words ever directed at me. Words that would make a hardened criminal blush.

Word after word fell like a lit match until the kindling of my own frustrations ignited, and the forest fire between us flamed. For the next hour of our drive, we unleashed every negative thought we had developed about the other, and not just insults, but full-on character assassinations. We were trying to inflict as much verbal pain on the other person as possible.

When I pulled up to the ranch, I had heard and said enough. All I wanted was to get away from Erin and run. Literally. The car had barely stopped before I sprang out, jetted to my camper, threw on my running clothes and shoes, put my journal in my running backpack, and started up a dirt road into the mountains.

I did not know where I was heading, but I ran with a fierceness that was uncommon for me. I was propelled from a place inside me that is rarely touched. One that needed to push hard against my physical limits to prove to myself that I could withstand the pain. That I could hold up under pressure. That there was at least one thing I could control. I lost time as I raced away from my emotions and what I thought was a failure of a relationship.

I'm not sure how long I ran, but at some point, intense thirst brought me out of the timeless void and back into the present. Slowing to a shuffle, I bent over, hands on my knees, and watched sweat fall to the bone-dry ground. This dirt road, this sun shining down on my back, this intense heat, made me feel alive. Happy to be here and totally spent.

Hearing a nearby creek, I quickly made my way to its bank and submerged my head. The cold rush of the mountain water flowing over my bald head poured life back into me. But after a minute, my John Muir moment passed, and the situation I was running from slammed into me. And it was something I had no answers for. On one hand, I truly wanted to marry Erin, but on the other, nothing in me desired to move forward. Deep inside, I realized we had issues that would not just disappear. Unfortunately neither of us knew how to deal with them. An impossible situation that seemed to provide no chance of a path forward.

As I sat there beside the creek, I pulled my journal from my backpack. Imagining myself as a modern-day John Muir, I wrote my thoughts.

> Lord, I am lost. I don't know what to do. I believed You were directing me to have Erin as my wife, but everything inside me seems turned upside down. We are saying the most horrible things to each other and about each other. And we are not just saying these things, we believe them. How can any of that be right? The very last thing I want to do is move forward into a marriage that seems destined to fail. I only want Your will, but I do not believe I can move forward with Erin, so I am going to call this off unless I hear directly from You. Lord, I am asking You to speak.

Later that evening, under cool clean sheets, as my mind drifted off to sleep, I was thinking about how we would break off the engagement.

My eyes popped open at 5:12 a.m., even before the light could bring back to life the previous night's death. As my feet hit the floor, I realized it was my birthday. My 30th birthday. Erin's 27th. The day that would go down as the day I broke off an engagement with a woman on her own birthday. Would this be a cruel or a welcome gift? My answer to this question was at least partially answered when I stepped outside to partake in the one legal substance that might actually help my mood. Coffee.

Stepping out of the camper to start my Jetboil for coffee, I stopped to breathe. The coolness of the mountain morning made me feel alive. As I waited on the water to boil, I sat on the picnic table then realized something was off. It was still quite dark, but it seemed like something obstructed my view. The more my eyes adjusted, I realized there was a poster hanging on a tree. I rolled my eyes. Great. Erin beat me to the punch and announced the calling off of our engagement via a poster. What a low blow.

Walking toward it, I saw the words Happy Birthday framing the top like an archway that welcomes you into the fair. Was this sincere, or a setup? What's that fine print underneath? Curiosity got the better of me, and I allowed my eyes to focus on the rest of the message under the archway. It simply read, I Love You.

Hmm. Am I willing to let my heart hope again?

Watching the morning light fill my surroundings, I contemplated that thought. After, I finished my coffee, then slowly made my way to our morning prayer meeting. Erin was, of course, the first person I saw. We were like two kids at a middle school dance, awkwardly avoiding each other while simultaneously trying to connect with each other. We exchanged birthday greetings, and

I thanked her for the poster. More awkward silence. Funny how words were in abundance yesterday in the car. Vicious words. Now we could barely string together a sentence for one another.

Luckily, the time of prayer and worship rescued us. The music soothed my mind as I sat on one of the couches and desperately sought the presence of God. The voices of my friends surrounded me and lifted me up. Maybe it was because it was our last day at camp together, but as soon as Erin and I started praying, our moods sweetened.

Shortly after we started, the leader of the prayer efforts for the camp, John, walked in. He didn't always join us for morning prayer, but I was glad that he was there for our last day. Over these two weeks, I had grown to admire John's spiritual maturity and genuine mentorship, not to mention his wisdom in all things marriage and manhood. His prayers were powerful as they breathed life into even the deadest of spiritual bones, and on this particular morning, I was carrying an entire cartload of dead bones that needed rattling.

About thirty minutes into the prayer time, we hit a moment when everyone was quiet and we simply rested in the Lord's presence. For some reason I opened my eyes and looked directly at John. Being of a larger build, and sitting there with his palms facing up, I smiled as I mused how much he resembled Buddha in that pose. At that moment, his eyes opened directly at me and his smile spread across his face as if he knew what I was thinking. Oh no, he's going to ask me to leave for not being spiritual enough. But apparently, he knew what someone else was thinking.

John had let us know on our first day that he believed God would sometimes provide words for him to share with others. He said he just wanted us to know in case it happened, as he knows not everyone has that same belief that God still does that sort of thing. When John had mentioned that, I hadn't thought much about it, as I was not completely sure I believed in that sort of thing either. However, John's next words would challenge that uncertainty.

"Thank you, Lord. You know I have wanted to share a word from You with Blake and Erin," he said. "Blake and Erin, I believe this is for you together. I don't know what this means, but I believe the Lord is telling you two to 'Forge Ahead.'"

When those last two words rolled off his tongue, I melted. I did not know what to do. I had never experienced anything like this before. I was not even sure I believed in words from God. My mind raced. Was I supposed to thank John? Should I walk over and give him a hug like after opening a Christmas present? Maybe I was supposed to lay down on the ground? Or kneel. I had seen people do that before. Maybe I was supposed to fall over? Was I supposed to give him a word back? If I messed it up, would the word be taken back? I just did not know.

It was like having the spiritual equivalent of wetting my pants in public. But then I felt another set of emotions filling me. I felt warmth, like I was standing in a warm bath and the water was quickly rising to cover my entire body until it stopped just below my chin. It was as if I was receiving the warmest hug I could possibly imagine. The realness of the Lord rested on me in a way that I have seldom experienced since.

Unless John had snuck into my camper the night before and read my journal, I knew there was no way he, nor anyone else, could have known the cries of my heart. The only logical conclusion was that there was really a God out there. A God who'd heard the cries of my heart. And not only had He heard, He'd answered me. He'd answered me in a way I could never have imagined possible. He'd answered me through a larger than normal, God-fearing, seventy-year-old Buddha lookalike I barely knew.

As that reality came to life inside me, I finally knew what one should do. Just receive the word. With that I simply sat there. Humbled. As the richness of this experience rested on me, I looked over at Erin and I knew that even with all the uncertainties, we were going to figure out how to be imperfect together. We just needed to have faith that the Lord would lead us to a better place than our current situation. We stared at each other. The water flowing from our eyes started to wash away the dirtiness of our yesterdays.

I may not have believed in this type of thing before, but I believed on this day.

The sounds of popping snapped me back to the hospital where the boy's and grandmother's family were cracking open those party poppers that have a bit of confetti and tiny prizes inside. How long had I sat there vicariously enjoying this birthday party?

Is Erin still napping, or does she need me? I should get back.

As I retraced my steps through the hospital corridor maze, I prayed under my breath, "Lord, I need some words from you now, like you spoke back then. I need you to strengthen me with hope to face the uncertainty ahead. You did it before…You can do it again."

CHAPTER TEN

Meaning

Some people spend Christmastime in a hospital. Of course, I knew this; but I didn't really know this until "some people" was us. While everyone else is bustling to shop, lace every edge of their homes with lights, attend holiday school concerts and beautiful church services, multitudes of families are fighting for their lives in hospitals. Peace on earth and joy to the world coexist with fear of losing loved ones and the heavy burden of illness. Maybe this juxtaposition is more present than we realize the other eleven months of the year, but in December, these realities stand side-by-side in stark contrast. Erin and I were living in both.

On the joy-to-the-world side, a steady stream of visitors blessed us with their presence, along with thoughtful gifts, inspirational cards, a Christmas tree, enough food and Santa-shaped cookies to feed the nursing staff, and a string of Rebekah's artwork to decorate the walls. Our friend, Matthew Calhoun, the one with crazy enough faith to believe we could actually make it to forty weeks, showed up to pray with us. Bursting in with a bouquet of flowers and a smile that could brighten the darkest of situations, Matthew also brought his hope-infused prayers which sustained us, even if just for a while.

On the heavy-burden-of-illness side, Erin's hematocrit levels were not holding steading. On Friday the numbers communicated that Erin's internal bleeding was not serious enough for our doctor to insist upon inducing labor. By Sunday the levels had dipped to a worrisome nineteen. The doctors ordered a blood transfusion. Three days into our new residence at the hospital, the prognosis did not appear to be moving in the right direction, but at least Baby Faith was still tucked inside Erin with a strong heartbeat. And other than the hematocrit drop, Erin claimed to feel just fine. It would've been nice to have these two sides remain balanced, equal in joy and burden.

Enter a neonatologist with her list of concerns. This doctor who specialized in the care of preemies was about to drop kick our joy/burden balance into the valley of the shadow of death.

Moments after doctors hooked Erin up to the blood transfusion IV, Dr. Happy (no, that was not her name, and yes, I am being sarcastic) rolled in like a brewing storm. Erin and I believed that our baby would stay in utero until she was full-term. But there was no way we were going to share these hopes with Dr. Happy. She wouldn't have been, well, happy about that.

"How has your Christmas season been going?" Erin asked cheerfully.

Dr. H's response was a blank stare.

"I've come here to discuss the situations that will most likely occur when a baby is born prematurely. You are at..." Dr. Happy checked her chart. "You are at twenty-two weeks and five days. Okay. Should your baby be born at this time, it would be considered a non-viable fetus with an infinitesimal chance of survival and therefore we would not perform heroic measures to try to save the baby. However, if you are able to make it until, perhaps, twenty-four or twenty-five weeks, there might be a chance of survival, but not without serious complications."

Erin's eyes hardened with defense. I knew my wife. Number one, she did not appreciate this doctor's refusal to see hope; and number two, never refer to her baby as a fetus.

Completely oblivious to Erin's change of expression, Dr.

Happy plowed ahead. "Preemies are monitored very closely as we watch for these common issues: brain bleeds, inability to digest food which leads to NEC, a common and often fatal condition as bacteria attacks the baby's intestines. Then there is the difficulty breathing, which requires us to intubate in order to increase oxygen levels; however, this can also be very damaging to the lungs and cause blindness. And then, even if the preemie does make it through the NICU, there are always the longer-term threats like Cerebral Palsy and others conditions like—"

"Excuse me," Erin said. "I think we've heard enough. We appreciate your time and hope you have a wonderful Christmas." Erin's blood was boiling, even the brand-new blood that was currently being transfused.

"Mrs. Hamby, I'm sorry if you don't want to hear all this, but we think it is important to make sure parents know the risks associated with these babies."

"Great. Consider us informed. We know there are risks, but what do you want us to do? Give up on fighting for our child simply because things could get challenging?"

"Well...I'm not suggesting that. We simply want you to understand that the path from here can be bleak."

"I guess that is a way to look at it," Erin said. "Another way might be to focus on the good things that could happen from here. We believe it's important to realize there is a human being inside me right now that has no ability to do anything for herself. We believe it is our job as parents, and frankly as human beings, to protect those who cannot protect themselves."

Dr. Happy remained emotionless, at least as far as I could tell. But Erin was just getting started.

"We know there are risks with our baby's future, but there are risks and uncertainty for our other daughter as well. For all of us. That doesn't mean we are going to focus on the bad that can happen. It means we are going to fight a little harder, believe a little deeper, and trust our God a little more. So, we appreciate you stopping by and letting us know these things. And we pray you have a great Christmas."

Now the doctor looked dazed, like an actor thrown off-script. With an "Okay" and a nod of the head, Dr. Happy exited as decisively as she had entered.

Before the door shut, I was already rustling through my bag of clothes.

"What are you doing, Sock?" Erin asked.

"I'm going for a run."

"It's 7:00 at night. And dark. And raining. You are not running outside. I need you to stay well."

"I'm not going to run outside."

"What does that mean? I'm sure they discourage running through the halls of the hospital."

By now I'd already slipped my running clothes on. "I'm going to go to the stairwell. It'll be fine, Erin, I just want to stretch my legs."

Guilt poured over me as I heard those last words. Stretch my legs? My wife had not left the bed in three days, was in the process of receiving a blood transfusion, and her life may or may not be hanging in the balance, and all I could think about was getting out of the room and stretching my legs? But my body had a mind of its own and my heart was along for the ride. Reaching for the door handle, I glanced back at Erin and felt such selfishness and weakness. Still, I left that last thought hanging in the doorway and literally ran out of the room.

Busting through the doors of Labor and Delivery, I pivoted a right then a quick left into the stairwell and bolted north. I ran like a fugitive being chased by his enemies through a deep forest. Only my enemies were words. Brain bleeds, the approaching hounds with their threatening growls. Blindness, the hidden potholes under my feet. Cerebral Palsy, the men with their pistols cocked. Death, the darkness of the night closing in on the chase. My thighs and lungs screamed with fire, but I could not stop running those stairs.

Why? Why were we doing this? Choosing a path for a baby who would probably suffer such terrible things? Was this because of our own selfish desire to have a baby, while forgetting about how our choices could forever impact Faith's life? Were we doing this out of some sort of self-righteous motivation to protect life while putting that very life in a situation where she might be subjected to so much pain that her life wasn't a true life at all? What even is a true life? A stair tripped me, and I clutched the banister to prevent slamming my head into the cement. But I could not stop. It was too dangerous to stop; too many words were hot on my heels. The more I ran, the further away I could get.

What about Rebekah? How would this impact her life? What about the practical side of raising a severely disabled child? The money, the time, the sacrifice for all of us? What would that do to our family? Our marriage? What about our hopes and dreams?

That last thought was an invisible wall slamming me to a stop in the middle of the stairwell. The ugliness of it. The selfishness of it. What kind of man, husband, and father was I to think such a terrible thought? The hurricane of emotions erupted from my gut and throat with a loud bellow that echoed through a dozen flights spinning up and down. I slammed my flat hand against the concrete wall, relishing the sting even as I crumpled to the ground and wept. The stairs were cold against my hot and fatigued body. My sobs deployed every bit of energy. I had nothing left.

Eventually, both my sobs and heavy breathing quieted. The silence in the stairwells rang in my ears. My thoughts had wrestled themselves to exhaustion and my lungs instinctively pulled in a deep sigh.

God. Please. What is going on? How can I feel this way? Help me find anything of worth or strength inside of me.

My ears sought the voice of God, hoping to detect audible words that would penetrate these concrete walls and breathe fresh life into my soul. But all I heard was my own steady breathing. My own heartbeat pounding.

Then some thoughts rose like the wisps of smoke from the beginning flames of a campfire. Thoughts that said:

Your questions are normal. Real. Human. Don't run from those questions. Instead, understand them and process them, and then don't absorb them. Let them go. You are not your every thought nor your doubts, and neither do your questions create and build your value or your character; rather, you are built by decisions, by actions.

Peace trickled into my soul, and I allowed this train of thought to guide me further.

Blake, it's not your job to decide if the life your child may or may not have is worth saving. Your job is to fight for her life, to work hard to give that life the best opportunity to thrive and to experience all the joys that life can bring. It's your job to stand up for your child when she cannot stand up for herself, and right now your baby, Faith, needs you to fight for her, to believe for her, and to pray for her - no matter the outcome.

Meaning

These silent truths continued to displace the deafening fears and lies that had been swirling in my head. The final thought that raised me back to my feet was this:

Every single life, every human being on this planet has worth and purpose. Even if that life has one breath or one billion. God sees every life, which He uniquely and masterfully crafted, and deeply loves. My role, not just as a parent, but as a fellow human being, is not to decide if a life is worth living, but to walk as Jesus did and work to bring honor, meaning, opportunity, and freedom to that life.

As I wove my way back through the corridors, I saw with fresh eyes each person I passed. Every one was made in the likeness and image of our God. Loved, treasured, and worthy. And when I re-entered our room, my eyes beheld my beautiful wife, graciously gazing back without the slightest bit of condemnation for abandoning her. She understood me better than I understood myself. I snuggled into bed next to her and thanked her for her strength and grace.

Erin welcomed me into her bed, held me, kissed me, then promptly instructed me to get out and take my sweaty self to the shower.

CHAPTER ELEVEN

Encouragers

Sitting at my office desk two days later felt surreal. The folders were exactly where I'd left them. My stapler, my pens, even my half-drunk cup of coffee, sat dutifully in their spots, unmoved from where they'd been before. Before. If only I could go back to before. How was it possible that before was only a few days ago? It felt like years. After a dazed several minutes, I dove into the work that needed to be completed before Christmas, and soon the rhythm of my job ushered my mind down a path of escape. A place of normalcy where I wasn't worried about my wife or my second child dying.

Hours slipped by before my phone buzzed with a text from my close friend Tanner.

: How's it going?

Great. Erin is feeling much better after the blood transfusion:

: I'm so glad! Do you need anything?

I think we're good for now. Thx so much :

: Here's the contact for Dr. Carlo. Call him.

A few years ago, Tanner and his wife, Lauren, had found themselves pregnant with not one, not two, not three, but four babies. When the quadruplets were born as preemies at The University of Alabama in Birmingham Hospital, one of the neonatologists who had cared for them was a man named Dr. Carlo. As highly as both spoke of him, I was surprised they didn't name one of their babies after him. Or all of them. Carlo. Carlos. Carolyn... The other night at the hospital when Tanner had visited me, he insisted I need to contact this miracle-working doctor. I decided to google the neonatologist.

A quick search of Dr. Carlo revealed that not only was he a neonatologist, but he appeared to be a big deal at UAB. UAB is a teaching hospital and the premier medical facility in Alabama. People travel from all over to come to UAB, and even though I'd never really thought about it much before, it dawned on me how beneficial it was to have world-class medical facilities in our hometown.

The more I read about Dr. Carlo, the more I questioned why in the world Tanner would have told me to call him. I was intimidated just reading his vitae, let alone calling the rockstar doctor out of the blue like he was my mother's best friend. Dr. Carlo had grown up and attended medical school in Puerto Rico, after which he'd moved to Cleveland to work at their Children's hospital. While there, he excelled at both his position at the hospital and his research regarding how best to care for preemie babies. He did so well, in fact, UAB had recruited him away. Here in Birmingham, he had helped design their NICU, led efforts to expand the NICU team, and was now leading the entire NICU staff.

In the safety of my office, I balanced my intimidation with my responsibility as a husband and a father. I thought, "It's not like a guy like that would answer, anyway. He'd have people to do that for him. Plus, my wife and baby were in a desperate condition... how can I not at least leave a message?" I picked up the phone and dialed.

"Hello."

Wait. Someone actually answered! My heart thumped in my chest. This had to be an assistant of his.

"Uh, Dr. Carlo please."

"Speaking."

"Oh, hello. Yes, thank you. I mean, hello. Right. Okay. Yes, my name is Blake Hamby, and my wife is in the hospital on bedrest with our second child who is currently just over twenty-two weeks, and our friends Brian and Lauren Tanner mentioned you had helped them, and we might want to call you to maybe, possibly, just ask you a few questions. But I can see you are very busy, so I will just reach out to your assistant and schedule some time to visit you, probably after the holidays?"

"Yes," Dr. Carlo said calmly. "I remember the Tanners. They had quads here a few years ago. Lovely couple. If you would like, we could either just talk now, or I could schedule some time for you to come by in the next few days. Which is best for you?"

"Okay. Sure. Please. Yes, I would like that." Why was I acting like a nervous schoolboy?

"So," he had a smile in his voice. "Would you like to ask me questions now, or would you like to come by?"

"Maybe that would be good. Yes, I will just ask you some questions now, sir, if that is acceptable to you?" Get yourself together, Blake! I took a deep breath to ready myself to ask the questions.

For the next twenty minutes, this very encouraging man answered every one of my questions and proved himself to be the absolute antithesis of the only other neonatologist I'd ever met, Dr. Happy. Speaking with confidence and encouragement, he shared the successes he had seen with babies born even at twenty-two weeks and how he was very willing to perform heroic measures to save their lives. He talked about the steroids Erin could get, the surfactant that would help when Faith was born, how the UAB team was structured, and finally, how parents could stay in the rooms with their preemie babies. He explained about how the delivery rooms were right next to the NICU so that the babies never were required to travel through unneeded spaces that might expose them to germs, how UAB had a doctor on site at all hours so that the mother did not have to wait until a specific doctor could get from their home to the hospital. He made me feel secure, like my wife and child had less of a chance of dying. But beyond all the information he shared, there was one unspoken thing he communicated loud and clear: Hope. Not only did he show me a way forward, he made it clear that we didn't need to be intimated.

As we hung up, Dr. Carlo insisted I take down his cell number and call him as things progressed. He also invited me to tour the NICU, which I replied I most certainly would take him up on. His last words to me in his beautiful Puerto Rican accent were that he would be praying for baby Faith.

Sitting in my office after the call, I thought I might have just spoken to an angel. Or maybe whatever is the next rank above an angel. Maybe I could talk Erin into naming our girl Faith Carlo?

Driving back to the hospital, I could not wait to tell Erin all about Dr. Carlo and UAB. Everything he had talked about, we needed. But that created a decision point. Should we stay at our current hospital, which had been good, or should we go? We were already at a great hospital, one that was taking great care of us. But was it good enough? Was there a better option? Would we be in better hands at UAB? Just imagining being cared for by the standards Dr. Carlo had described filled my heart with such hope... that is, until another thought popped my hope balloon before it could even rise far off the ground. UAB was out-of-network for our health insurance.

My job just happens to be in insurance, so I realized if we went to an out-of-network facility and this baby came early, it could mean bankruptcy. But how could I place a dollar amount on the life of my wife and child? I didn't even have to consider the answers to that question. Yes. Yes. A thousand times, yes. If bankruptcy is what it meant, then bankruptcy it would be.

So which is the right choice? What if one or both of them died because we weren't in the right hospital? These questions swirled around me and whipped the fresh air of hope Dr. Carlo had offered my mind into a turbulent storm. I bounded the steps two at a time to our hospital room #307 hoping Erin would bring calm. We needed answers. We needed to figure this out. Now.

"Erin," I said urgently as I swooped into the room. "We have to talk."

"Hey, Sock! Guess what time it is?"

"It's time for us to talk. We have a very important decision to make."

"It's almost cleaning time!" Erin said, seemingly not hearing my plea.

Cleaning time. Knowing this trumped any attention I could expect from my wife, so I plopped down in my chair. Cleaning time had become Erin's favorite part of the day during the last few days of her hospital stay. Silly as having clean floors and empty trash cans might seem, especially in light of the heavy situations we faced from day to day, this fifteen minutes was much more than just cleaning. It had become an oasis in the middle of a Sahara, a time when negativity and fear were swept out and positivity and hope were swept in. And it was all because of Gloria.

Gloria was an older Black lady, and while she never spoke specifics of it, both Erin and I perceived that life and people had treated her less than fairly on more than a few occasions. Even so, each day she came into our room wearing a beautiful smile that glowed even brighter when she greeted us.

"How's my little mamma doing today? You keeping that baby all tucked in and warm in that tummy of yours?" Her voice sang like a grandma rocking her grandchild to sleep on a warm Alabama night, with the summer cicadas singing along.

"Yes, ma'am," Erin said. "I sure am trying."

"Well good. That's just what I want to hear. You know, we

already had one miracle baby born at Christmas, and I sure am thankful for Him. So we don't need another. I would just as soon have that precious little one you got cooking in there stay put for a bit longer." She focused her eyes on Erin's belly and said, "You hear that, little baby girl? You stay right where you are until God says so!"

How was it that when Miss Gloria spoke, it was more like a declaration of faith? Like she was calling things into being?

"I'm with you Miss Gloria. I agree."

"You gonna be all right, sugar," she smiled. "You gonna be just fine. And you know how I know that?"

I jumped into the conversation because I really wanted to know how she knew. She'd only known us for a few days, so how could she have such unshaken confidence?

"How do you know that, Miss Gloria?" I asked.

After looking deeply into my desperate eyes, she shifted her glance over to the corner of Erin's bed where her Bible sat.

"Because of that right there. Every day I come in here to clean this room a bit, I see that Bible by you. And it's not just setting there collecting dust, either. It's being used." Gloria pointed to the nightstand. "You got them note cards beside you with Bible verses, it's opened to a different place each day, and I can see it on your face. That book there is a changing you. So if you just keep on looking at it and look a little less at them monitors, you gonna be just fine."

This was the type of conversation Gloria brought with her every day. Words of faith sprinkled between her soulful singing as she cleaned our room. Those fifteen minutes were the best of our day. Funny how the best medicine we received wasn't administered by a doctor or nurse but by the person tasked with cleaning our room. Maybe she knew she needed to rid the room of not just the trash or the dust that collected in the corner, but something much different. Something that could not be picked up with a hand or swept with a broom. Maybe it was all the uninvited darkness that came into hospital rooms that she knew were the most important to clean out. Things like despair. Hopelessness. Fear. Loneliness. Brokenness. Intimidation.

I'm not sure where she'd learned how to remove the darkness, but I know she dispensed medicine critical to our chances of survival.

Gloria hummed a low hymn as she pushed her cleaning cart toward our door. When her humming stopped, I looked up to see she'd halted before exiting our room, and she turned around and met my eyes.

"Don't you worry, son. You don't need to have everything figured out because the Lord already does. You just need to trust."

My breath caught in my chest, and my eyes burned. How did she know?

I sat there realizing I had just had two encounters with an angel on the same day. First, Dr. Carlo and now this precious woman. Maybe I could talk Erin into naming our girl Faith Carlo-Gloria?

CHAPTER TWELVE
Nightmares

My eyes popped open to the sound of alarms. What time is it? More nurses than I could count rushed in and surrounded our hospital bed. What day is it?

"You need to get out of the bed right now, Mr. Hamby," a nurse ordered.

I didn't recognize anyone in our room.

"She's hemorrhaging," another nurse said.

"Mama, what's wrong?"

How did Rebekah get to the hospital? Why was she standing there in her pajamas?

A nurse ripped back the covers to reveal an enormous amount of blood surrounding my dead wife.

"Mama!" screamed Rebekah.

I shot up in bed to dark silence. Trying to catch my breath, I rose from my couch bed and yanked the sheets off Erin. There was not enough light to see, so I grabbed my phone and tapped on the flashlight.

"Blake, what are you doing?" Erin did not appreciate the wake-up call.

No blood. Just a hellish nightmare.

I fell onto the couch and drew the covers around my shoulders. "I'm sorry." I spoke smoothly, trying to hide my panic. "Go back to sleep."

"Sock, you're shivering," she said as she drifted back to sleep. "Snuggle in next to me and get warm."

I climbed in, even though my shaking had nothing to do with being cold. Within seconds, Erin's breath was slow and deep, and I lay there listening hard to every breath, wondering if they might be her last.

"Everything is going so much better," I reassured myself. "Erin's hematocrit numbers are steady, the baby's heartbeat continues to stay strong, and the doctor even mentioned the possibility of us going home soon so Erin could finish out her bedrest there. There is no reason to worry about Erin dying."

But that wasn't the full truth, was it? There was a substantial risk, or we wouldn't be here in the first place. Dr. Stephens would never have suggested induction, knowing our baby would never survive, if we were not in a life-or-death situation. There wouldn't be a need for blood transfusions if there was no internal bleeding. If Erin's life was not at risk, then we could walk out of here right this second.

"Jesus," I whispered. "I need your peace."

I could still hear the thumping of my heartbeat through the pillow, alternately praying for Erin and the baby and then praying for my own peace. I would be lying if I didn't mention that the images of my nightmare tapped on my shoulder like an incessant child demanding attention. For hours my mantra was Isaiah 26:3–4, *"You will keep in perfect peace, those whose minds are steadfast because they trust in you. Trust in the Lord forever, for the Lord, the Lord himself is the Rock eternal,"* alternating with an old Irish proverb that goes something like, "Ninety-nine bottles of beer on the wall, take one down." Over and over, I muttered these words as a means to either shield me from my fears or drown them.

"Good morning." Sweet words from my wife pulled me out of a restless slumber.

As my eyes adjusted to the morning light, I noticed Erin peacefully sitting next to me in bed with her open Bible, the picture of serenity as the first rays of sun glowed around her. How was she able to stay so deeply rooted in contentment and safety? Her faith and strength inspired me as she continued to dive so deep into the Lord's presence that the storm raging around her was unable to touch her. Meanwhile that same storm continued to haunt me in the light of day. If I lost Erin, how would I cope?

"Are you ready for our morning ritual?" she asked.

Ever since that first morning when we'd buoyed our souls by singing "God is Able" and reading Psalm 91, we had not skipped a day. This time of devotion to God and to each other had become necessary spiritual food to help our faith grow. Not wanting Erin to worry about me, I decided to leave last night's terror at the door as we entered our safe place. With each phrase of the song and Psalm, my soul settled and fell in step with my wife's path of hope and courage.

"When do you want to put the brisket in?" Erin smiled after our worship time was over.

"What do you mean?" And then the realization hit me. "It's Christmas Eve!"

A long-standing Blackstone-Hamby Christmas tradition, grafted in from Erin's mom, is a scrumptious South Louisiana Cajun feast: dripping brisket rounded out with spinach madeleine, corn maque choux, mirliton, and more rice than humanly possible to eat. And the pièce de résistance—carafes filled with spicy brisket gravy to douse everything with, save the pecan pie. Just thinking about that meal made me excited.

"I never imagined, in a million years, we would spend our holidays in the hospital," I said.

"You know what?" Erin answered. "I wouldn't have either. But I have to admit, I'm kind of thankful for this time."

I blinked, wondering if she'd lost her mind, but she just smiled. "No seriously, Sock. I'm not sure I've ever felt so rested. These last nine days, when all I've had to focus on is rest and prayer and each other, I consider it a gift. It's been the most peaceful Christmas, where we can celebrate the meaning of the season instead of shopping. I've never felt so close to God as He has walked every step with me. And I've never felt so close to you either."

Closing my eyes and taking a deep breath, I considered her words. There was more truth in them than I had allowed myself to process. Save the nightmare several hours ago, there had been many blessings in this storm. An intangible strength from the Lord that undergirded even my frequent freak-outs. The steady stream of friends and family with gifts of prayer, cards, gifts, texts, and most of all, their time. Our parents who unquestionably and generously took care of Rebekah every day while we lived in Room 307. The countless small acts of kindness added up to a fortress of community and support. How would I have known these blessings had life stayed the normal course I nostalgically longed for? But while I treasured these blessings, I'm not sure I wouldn't, in a heartbeat, exchange them for the security of knowing my wife and baby were back on the normal course where nine months fly by and a healthy, full-term baby is the prize.

"Erin, thank you for seeing this through the eyes of faith. You don't know how much your perspective means to me." I gathered her in my arms and kissed her, then whispered in her ear, "I have never felt so close to you or loved you more than this moment right here."

I drank in the atmosphere of gratitude and love until...

"Erin."

"Yes?"

"It's Christmas Eve."

She chuckled, "I think we just established that."

"No. I mean, we haven't even shopped for Rebekah! We don't have anything under that tree for her to open!" I motioned to our tiny Christmas tree the Tanners had brought to our room, the tree that had equally tiny presents sitting under it.

"Honey, she's so little, it'll totally be okay if she—"

"No. It's not okay," I insisted. "I need to do this. Listen, I'm going to run to work for an hour or so to close up business that needs to be done before Christmas, and then I'm getting a few things. Can you please jot down a short list of what I should get?

Then I'll zip around to pick those up before my parents bring her here tonight?"

Erin knew me well enough to know this "need" of mine was my way of controlling what was in my grasp to control, my way of trying to make up for the insurmountable things I had no way of controlling. She grabbed a pen and paper. Smiling at me, she assured me, "You get ready, and I'll have a list for you before you go."

CHAPTER THIRTEEN
It's a Wonderful Life

Downtown Homewood was a Christmas wonderland. As I turned the corner onto 18th Street, the social center of my little neighborhood city, I felt my heart swell with pride that this was my community. We knew how to do Christmas right. Every storefront dripped in gorgeous décor, the light posts swirled with garland and lights, and Christmas music piped in from every corner. The vibe was magical, and for a moment, I was swept into a world of good cheer and anticipation, along with a nagging feeling that this reminded me of something.

Nothing short of a miracle, I found one vacant parking spot right in the street's hub, probably the only open spot for at least a half mile, both ways.

Then I remembered. Bedford Falls! This whole vibe felt like I'd just stepped foot into one of my favorite Christmas movies of all time: It's a Wonderful Life. Bedford Falls is the fictional city from It's A Wonderful Life and the home of George Baily. George longed his entire life to get out of that little town. However, he never left because life continued to give him new twists that derailed his plans. All the twists eventually brought him to a faithful Christmas Eve when his whole world seemed to come crashing down over him. Sitting in my car, I felt like I could relate to George.

I also remember how George dealt with his crisis. He found a bar, got drunk, jumped in a freezing river and then God sent a quirky old angel to help him find his path back to his life that had more meaning than he realized. Sitting there in my car I thought about how I knew where a bar was in my town. And while we did not have any freezing rivers, I figured I could sneak into the community swimming pool and jump off the diving board. Maybe that would get the Lord's attention and He would send a quirky angel to make my situation all better. Or, I remembered the angel said that every time you hear a bell ring an angel gets his wings. Maybe I could start with simply finding a bell and ringing it just to see if anything happens.

Realizing neither of those were the best solution, I decided to get out of my truck. As I opened the door, I took it all in. Families were everywhere, buzzing in and out, laughing and chattering about the normal Christmas things. Probably kids asking if Santa would come tonight or in the morning. Husbands asking when the in-laws would arrive, and then when they would leave. Wives checking the lists to make sure there were no last-minute gifts still to purchase. I searched these parents' happy faces and imagined they were just as excited as their children to open gifts, to hear the delight as each kid ripped open their boxes.

Then I thought about all those families and how I assumed not one of their conversations consisted of worries about how to celebrate Christmas with a toddler in a hospital room with a couple of poorly wrapped, haphazard presents under a janky tree with colored blinking lights, or of a mom in a bed who may or may not be bleeding internally while her baby in utero hung on somewhere between life and death. And for good measure, my imagination threw in any number of permanent disabilities this unborn child would inherit due to no fault of her own. Oh yeah, and there was no Christmas brisket either. For the first time in my life, I think I understood George Bailey and why he wanted to hurl himself off that bridge.

Stuffing those thoughts under a stiff upper lip, I ordered myself to just find the presents and get back to the hospital.

Walking into the Homewood Toy Store, I was reminded how much Rebekah loved this place. Every aisle showed her wonders she'd never seen before, and she'd giggle with every surprise. My eyes puddled as my heart ached to hear my daughter's sweet giggle.

Blake, get yourself together. Just get the stuff on the list and be done.

These were the items Erin had written: a doll with matching pajama sets for both the doll and Rebekah, and a pop-up Christmas themed book. Finding the doll section was easy, but deciding upon which one to buy seemed impossible. Do I pick one that looks as close to Rebekah as possible, or do I go for variety? Would she want the matching pajamas to be a nightgown or one with pants and a shirt? How was I supposed to know which is the right one? If I couldn't even pick out the right doll for my daughter, how could I be trusted to make the right medical choices for my wife and baby? Should we stay at the hospital we are at or go to UAB where Dr. Carlo and his experts might give us better care? Should I rely on our insurance or risk our financial future to go with an out-of-network hospital? My mind swirled with the unknowns. I grabbed a doll, the nearest pajama set in Rebekah's size, and marched toward the books.

Just pick something and get out of here.

It's a Wonderful Life

So that's what this Christmas has come to? Mindlessly grabbing gifts, throwing them in bags, and tossing them under a tree? This eighteen-inch doll is taller than the tree itself. Nice. That's gonna look awesome to have the little tree standing on top of the doll box. What kind of provider am I that I couldn't have thought ahead to plan a proper Christmas for my family?

Not having the mental margin to find the pop-up book section, I surrendered my inner male aversion to asking for directions at all costs and recruited a toy store employee to direct me to an entire section of children's pop-up books. Who knew there would be so many? Why were there that many choices? I pulled out every Christmas-ish title and slunk down into a child-sized chair that made me feel like a gawky Will-Ferrell-like giant in Elf, but without all the hope, joy, and laughter. Remembering his mantra that the "best way to spread Christmas cheer is singing loudly for all to hear," I considered breaking into song.

That was when I realized there already was a song trilling over the loudspeaker. What is that song playing in this store? Erin and I were Christmas music junkies and had every album from Bing to Maria to Bieber, and this was one I'd never heard before. Crouched on my pink child-sized chair, I strained to hear the lyrics. The country song was describing a boy tugging on the sweaters of people at the mall asking where the line was for Jesus, if Christmas was His birthday. As the song progressed, maybe it was the tiny chair, or maybe it was how tiny I felt against my looming circumstances, but I felt like that little boy searching for Jesus throughout a too big world. Christmas was a time to celebrate God's greatest gift to us, a Savior who promised to never leave or forsake us. But I couldn't seem to find Him. My heart was unraveling. So much for all that nonsense about singing loudly to bring Christmas cheer.

Then I heard the last lyric of the song: "Where's the line to see Jesus? He was born for me. Santa gave me presents, but Christ gave His life for me."

With those last words, me heart fell like a toddler just learning to walk. I folded my arms across my knees and rested my forehead against them. I longed for my journal to write the words that needed to be said. Instead I continued to bury my head deeper into my knees and pray. Jesus, help me. Help my faith. I'm struggling to make sense out of all of this, and I feel like I'm not enough. Maybe I'm not enough...but You are more than enough. You gave Your life for me, and in my heart, I know that if You would go to that extreme for me, You give even more than I can imagine to help me lead my family through this very difficult time. I need to know You are here with me.

It felt good to pray. To just be real.

"Excuse me, son?"

Before looking up, my mind flashed an image of a bird's eye

view of what I must look like just now. A grown man in a suit crunched up on a preschooler's pink chair, head in his lap, a doll by his side, and pop-up books strewn around him. Maybe if I don't move, the other man will think I am a mannequin and just leave.

"Son?"

My eyes lifted and met a pair of the kindest and wisest eyes. A gentleman, maybe in his late sixties, sat down next to me in the other pre-school chair.

"Are you waitin' for your wife, too?" he chuckled. "I vowed last year that Anna and I would not wait until the last minute to buy for the grandkids, but here we are again."

I don't know why I did it. I'm not that guy. But I couldn't help myself; his kind eyes seemed to draw the words right out of me. I spilled my guts. All of them. From my fears about Erin dying and about my unborn child, to my failure of knowing which hospital we should be in, to my inability to pick out the right doll and pop-up book for my firstborn girl. I might have also told him about my love for It's a Wonderful Life, and my unnatural obsession with our annual Cajun Christmas brisket and gravy. I might have even asked him to sing with me to see if Will Ferrell knew what he was talking about.

This man seemed to understand. The compassion in his eyes spoke volumes and somehow sharing that moment strengthened me. I wasn't alone. This stranger was in it with me. And even though I didn't have any answers, right in that moment, I knew I was going to be okay.

Without a word, he picked up the doll, the pajamas, all three of the books, and walked away. For a second, I thought all his compassion was just an act to steal the presents I had for his grandchildren. But moments later, he came back with all the presents for Rebekah packaged and paid for.

"Sir," I protested. "I can't let you…I mean, I don't need you to—"

With a flick of his hand, he waved away my words.

"Son, trust me when I say that I understand. I've been where you are today…at Christmas time, to boot, about thirty years ago. Hardest time in my life. I just needed to know that God saw me, that He was with me, that I was gonna make it. Time and time again, He sent me people to reassure me like that angel did for George Bailey." He smiled. "It's one of my favorite movies, too. And someday, long after you and your family have walked through this tough season with God's strength, you're gonna be talkin' to a young man who needs to know that God sees him." He put his hand on my shoulder and a warmth filled my heart. "Merry Christmas, son."

As this man walked away to join his wife's bustling around the toy store, I swear I heard a bell ring.

CHAPTER FOURTEEN

Christmas

Christmas morning arrived as gentle as new fallen snow. It was as if the opening lines of "Twas a Night Before Christmas" had snuck into our room last night and snuggled up beside us. Not a creature was stirring, not even a nurse. To have the luxury of sleeping in while living in a hospital, without being awakened by people poking and prodding, was as rare as a Christmas snowfall in Alabama.

Erin had been progressing so well there were no vitals to check, no blood tests to draw, no discouraging conversations to have.

With a heart filled with gratitude, I scanned our room, occupied only by my slumbering family. My wife, our firstborn, our soon-to-be second born, and me. Peace. The only details that could've made the setting more Christmassy would have been a donkey, a manger, and a few wise guys bringing us presents. Then again, we did have the one wise man who generously bought Rebekah's gifts in the toy store last night.

His wonderful act of kindness had filled our Christmas Eve with more hope than I'd felt for weeks. From the moment my parents had brought Rebekah to our room, all seemed right in the world. Even the dry meatloaf and mashed potato takeout dinners from the hospital cafeteria seemed good. Rebekah giggled at the big presents "under" the tiny tree, and it was a joy to watch her open each one. Erin and I were experiencing a peace with Jesus like we'd never had before. All our preconceived notions of what a perfect Christmas should look like, all the food, the games, the parties, were overshadowed with our stripped-down version in Room 307. Hamby party of three, soon to be four, was more than enough, and we drank up every moment like a cup of eggnog beside a warm fire.

About lunch time an old familiar voice rumbled in my belly. Hungry was reminding me he needed attention, and while our options for a Christmas spread worthy of a Hallmark movie were still nonexistent, my spirit was strong enough to face the realization that God and I could conquer anything, even if the meatloaf dinner was still the special downstairs. As I laced Rebekah's shoes, I heard carols being sung in the hallway. Peeking out our door, the delicious smells brought a deep burn from my stomach.

A family dressed in their Sunday best carried more food containers than a Tupperware convention. After they finished their chorus of "Joy to the World," the mother spoke to the medical staff and the other curious faces poking out of their rooms.

"Merry Christmas from the Carter family! A few years ago, we found ourselves right here throughout the Christmas holidays, fighting for our daughter's life. We were so consumed with the issues of each day, celebrating Christmas wasn't even on the table. Literally. It never crossed my mind, or my husband's to plan for any kind of meal that we had for years made a holiday tradition. I guess that's the kind of thing we take for granted until the moment it's not there. That Christmas afternoon as we sat alone in our hospital room eating dried cafeteria leftovers out of small cardboard boxes, we made a promise we would never forget how that moment felt…and that we would help other families not have to go through Christmas without a proper Southern meal."

A stunned moment of silence filled the hallways as my heart melted like snow at the thought of this family's generosity. How many hours had it taken them to cook all these meals? How much money? The deep burn from my stomach was eclipsed by the tears burning my eyes, and as my gaze met the other families in the rooms next to ours, their faces mirrored mine. One husband, about six doors down, started clapping, which set off an eruption of cheers and applause and quite a few tears.

Love can feel like so many things. A kiss from a spouse. A daughter's tiny arms tightly hugging your neck. An encouraging text during a challenging time. A neighbor selflessly mowing your lawn. On this Christmas day, love felt like platefuls of spicy ham, all the fixin's, and a blanket of gravy poured over it all. Families from our floor, as well as doctors and nurses, lingered together for the next hour as we shared and laughed at Christmas memories, filled our plates with seconds and thirds, and finally with hearts more stuffed with love than our stomachs with food, if that were possible, each family carried our own personalized platter of desserts to each of our rooms. The Carter family loved us so well, none of us will ever forget it.

Later that cold but warm Christmas day, snuggled deeply in our hospital beds, Erin and I whispered our prayers of thanks to our God, who supplied us with more than we could ever have imagined. Erin shared with me that if God was so rich in mercy to supply the details of our Christmas, the presents and the food, how much more could we trust Him to be more than enough for whatever lay ahead? I held her, hoping to absorb by osmosis her overflowing and unshakable faith.

CHAPTER FIFTEEN

Moving On

The next few days were not much different from our peaceful Christmas Day. Erin remained stable, Faith seemed to be holding her own inside Erin's tummy, and I had not experienced any major freak-out moments in at least a few days. All things considered, life was moving upward.

As the New Year approached, conversations about us going home were as common as conversations about the University of Alabama and LSU's upcoming rematch in the National Championship game. While both were exciting discussions, both brought me their own level of anxiety. As a Southerner and a graduate of the University of Alabama, college football admittedly carries a little too much weight in my soul. As a husband and dad, my highly sophisticated research regarding placenta abruptions which I had conducted through Google, brought a more meaningfully and honorable weight to my soul. Through my research, I'd learned that the placenta does not reattach itself to the uterine wall. Soooo...basically the placenta was still hanging on by a thread that at any moment could completely detach, which could mean Faith would need immediate help to have any possibility of survival, and it could also cause Erin to bleed out internally.

The decision from the doctors to release us was as inevitable as the kickoff to the National Championship game. Erin was springing this coop. So, on December 29, exactly two weeks after we had taken up residence in the hospital, we were paroled.

Scanning our room to make sure we hadn't left anything behind, I leaned against the doorframe with a conflicted heart. Even Erin was sad to leave. How could this now empty room have possibly, just moments ago, been stuffed with the life-altering experiences and memories of our last two weeks? Strangers had become family. Friends and relatives had poured out their love and support onto Erin and me. And just like that, we were turning a page on a very special, albeit unwanted, chapter of our lives.

We were living out song lyrics I had heard at a few too many taverns, more times than seemed respectable: "You don't have to go home, but you can't stay here."

CHAPTER SIXTEEN

Familiar Faces

Deep sleep can cover with a fog even the most obvious of situations.

"Wake up." Was this happening in a dream, or was this Erin? "Blake, are you awake?" It was Erin. What day was it? Friday. January 6. Was I late for work? No. It's still dark outside.

I rolled back over as I muttered, "Hmmm. Let's just go back to sleep."

"I wet the bed."

Propping myself up on my elbow, I responded with a laugh.

"What's with you being pregnant and wetting the bed?" In her second trimester carrying Rebekah, Erin and I had taken a getaway to The Grove Park Inn in North Carolina and while watching a late-night comedy, we had laughed so hard she'd wet the bed, which only made us laugh harder.

"Don't make me laugh." She had giggled. "You know I can't handle it. I need you to help me get up."

For the last week the doctors had given strict bedrest instructions for Erin. Horizontal only, except for necessary trips to the bathroom.

Staggering the five feet to the bathroom to get things ready, I stopped at the sink to splash some water on my face. As I wiped off the water, still smiling about Erin's incontinence, the fog dissolved. And so did my smile. My heart sank as I realized Erin probably did not wet the bed. Her water had broken. At twenty-five weeks of gestation. Staring at my reflection in the mirror, I questioned if the man I saw was ready for what was going to happen next.

After a quick conversation to convince Erin that her water had broken, we were in the car, speeding yet again to the hospital. Thankfully my parents had moved into our house during Erin's bedrest, so that we'd be able to leave at any time, knowing that Rebekah was in excellent hands.

Wheeling into the very familiar parking lot, I wondered how

many more times we were going to be able to do this before our life's plane crashed. Erin's water breaking as we entered the twenty-fifth week of gestation did not make me feel like we had much more runaway to deal with.

The nurses whisked us to a room we had never visited before, one that didn't offer a warm and fuzzy feeling, one used to perform emergency c-sections. After the standard blood pressure checks, IV insertions, and normal assessment questions, we found ourselves entering another episode of the Waiting Game. It felt more like learning to stand in an eye of a hurricane, with no knowledge of what category storm was coming. What would the collateral damage be? One life? Two lives? What if this was one of the last times Erin and I would be together on this side of heaven? I drank in every last second.

Not knowing how to put into words the worry and terror and love that I felt for her, I looked into her eyes and said, "Have I told you lately that I love you?"

Erin scrunched her eyebrows. "Did you just quote Michael Bolton?"

I played it off. "I'm just so glad to be right here with you." Please, please, don't die, is what I wanted to say.

"Me, too, Sock." Erin took a deep breath and closed her eyes. She didn't seem to have even the slightest thought that trouble was ahead. Meanwhile, my mind was Simone Biles performing her floor routine. The thoughts tumbled out of my mouth.

"Erin, I want you to know that if tomorrow never comes...I hope you know how much I love you. I hope you know how I have really tried in every way, to show you every day, that you're my only one. And if your time on earth is through, and I have to face this world without you, the love you have given me in the past, I want you to know it will be enough to last."

Erin's eyes popped open. "Blake, what are you talking about? Now you're quoting me Garth Brooks?"

"No. No, of course not." I was quickly ruining our Hollywood version of a final farewell. "Okay. Well. Maybe. I just want you to know that you are amazing. And how you have loved me is enough, and we'll be good. Because you have loved us so well. I mean, I love you. And I thank you. No, I don't mean that. Yes, no, I actually do mean that but what I really mean is—"

"Blake," Erin smiled and closed her eyes again. Why is she not in the least bit freaking out? "You need some coffee. Why don't you go get some Starbucks?" She squeezed my hand. "I am not going to die. Both Faith and I are going to be fine. I know in my heart that God is in control and because of that, I am good. You are good...Now go and get a coffee." As I kissed her forehead, she added, "And Sock, you never need to steal words from Bolton or Brooks. I know you love me, and I hear it more in the way you love me than the words you say."

Walking out the door, I thought how imperfectly perfect Erin was for me, which triggered the image of life without Erin. The thought wrestled the breath from my lungs. Thankfully the image was quickly pinned to the mat by my friend Tanner, standing in the hallway with two Starbucks coffees in his hands.

"What are you doing here?" I smiled, taking one of the coffees.

"I came to check on my buddy."

"But how did you know where we were?"

"Dude, you texted me this morning letting me know y'all were headed here and asked for prayers."

I really did need coffee; I'd forgotten all about the texts I'd sent to friends and family.

"The doctors are pretty sure her water broke, and now they are setting her up for a magnesium drip to try to hold off any contractions. We'll see where we go from here."

Tanner wrapped his arms around my shoulders and said, "God's got this. Just trust Him."

In those six little words, Tanner said so much. He'd warred through this battle with his own wife and kids, and he'd lived to tell about the wonders of God. He understood exactly what we were facing, and I was grateful he was in my corner, battling with me and holding up my arms.

Tanner stayed with Erin and me until the doctors were certain the baby was not quite ready to come. The nurses checked us into the hospital and then the orderly wheeled us right back into Room 307! We were back home.

"See, Sock?" Erin said, grinning. "What are the chances we'd be in the exact same room? This is God showing us that He cares about the details. How much more will He take care of both Faith and me?"

While the images of Erin's placenta ripping to the point of no return continued their mental onslaught of harassment, I had to admit she had a point.

CHAPTER SEVENTEEN

Game Time

Morning dawned on Saturday, and almost as bright as the sun rising was the arrival of Erin's sister Ashley who had hopped on a plane to be with us. Erin could not have been more excited to see "Tootie," as the family nicknamed her. Also adding to the comfort of the weekend was the ESPN coverage for the college football National Championship game. Alabama was scheduled to play LSU in New Orleans the upcoming Monday. For Alabama fans, this was the equivalent of the Pope and Billy Graham both speaking at a rally with Zac Brown singing the National Anthem and Lynyrd Skynyrd closing with an acoustic playing of "Amazing Grace" and "Sweet Home Alabama." Before life interrupted, Erin and I had planned on attending the monumental game. This was the kind of weekend that dominates every sports radio talk show South of DC from August to December, and the kind of match-up all respectable Southerners, both young and old, dream about late on Saturday evenings in the fall. But, thanks to so many things out of our control, here we were in good ol' Room 307 with very different plans for the weekend.

Listening to the familiar voices of Kirk Herbstreit, Desmond Howard, Lee Corso, Chris Fowler, Sam Ponder, and the rest of the gang provided a nice level of coziness for Erin and me because we normally started every Saturday in the fall with their voices guiding us through another glorious day of college football. Just their presence on our hospital TV made us both feel as if things were not as dire as they otherwise might seem.

As the crisp January day slowly turned the page into a frigid January evening, the three of us settled in for the night. Blair, one of our favorite nurses who cared for us during Christmastime, was kind enough to find a rollaway bed for Tootie so we could make a slumber party out of it. In their final checks for the night, Blair and her assistant half-jokingly and half-seriously commented that it was expected to be a busy night, due to the full moon.

"Is that a real thing?"

"Absolutely!" They both chimed at the same time.

"No, seriously," Blair said. "For whatever the reason, activity in labor and delivery picks up on nights like this. It happens every full moon."

I chuckled the statements away, thinking that old wives' tale was a bit too fantastical for me. Once the nurses left and the three of us were alone, we talked and laughed until we began to drift to sleep.

Just about the time Tootie and I entered into our rest, Erin whispered, "Hey guys. I need you to help me get to the potty."

"Are you sure?" I asked. "You really shouldn't get up."

"I really need to go," she insisted.

Tootie and I begrudgingly helped Erin gently swing from her bed to the stool toilet the nurses had set beside her bed. We reminded her not to strain at all, just to allow her body to release on its own. Erin looked uncomfortable, and Tootie and I exchanged concerned looks, realizing this might not be a good thing.

"Erin," I said, "I think we need to call the nurses."

"Why, so they can watch me poo? No thanks. It's hard enough trying to concentrate with the two of you watching me."

While I agreed she had a point, I took the risk to overrule her and hit the nurse's call button. The last thing I wanted after all this time was to have our second born drop into a toilet. Certainly that would not line up with best practices for delivering a micro preemie.

Blair, who just moments earlier was all smiles and jokes quickly became focused. She very kindly, but very directly, told Erin to lay back down in the bed. Erin was in labor.

The room transformed before our eyes from a sweet slumber party into the hospital version of a NASCAR pit stop. Nurses seemed to multiply at the same level as my anxiety. At one point five nurses crowded around us, each flurrying with a different objective. Just when my knees buckled under my swirling emotions, nurses levered Erin's bed into a rolling bed and started to wheel her out of the room.

I froze. I needed to go with her, but my legs wouldn't move. My catatonic state did not last long as nurse Blair looked at me and ordered, "Dad, come on!" That command would have made Patton proud. My legs didn't dare disobey.

As I was leaving our room Tootie grabbed my hand, and I looked her in the eye and asked her to pray. As I finished those words and stepped into the hall, I plunged into a raging river of emotions. Only time would tell if the currents would lead me toward one of the greatest adventures I would ever have or a catastrophic event that I was not prepared to handle.

After a few quick bends in the river, I stepped into a holding room. Like an eddy before a big rapid, it provided a safe place to scope out the dangerous torrents we were about to enter. Through a partially opened door to my left, a flurry of activity flowed around my wife. Blair was still with me but she was needed in the mix of commotion in the other room.

"Hang tight." She tried to comfort me, and dove into that room, shutting the door behind her.

All alone, I pictured terrorizing scenarios, from Erin bleeding out, to her going into hysterics, to Faith being born horribly deformed. I could not stop the current of images. I saw myself weeping over my wife's dead body, having to tell my family, raising Rebekah all on my own. I'm not sure how long this went on; it could have been five minutes or thirty minutes. Then Blair shouted, "Dad!" Pulling myself to her attention, a blue mass was hurdled at me. "Put this on. You're in the game. Let's go!"

I walked robotically into the maelstrom of the operating room. Doctors and nurses surrounded the bottom half of my wife, and I dared not look too closely; seeing a hole cut into Erin's stomach would probably send me to the floor.

Jesus, help me be the man she needs me to be.

"Hey," I smiled. "Fancy meeting you here."

"Where have you been?"

"Oh, ya know"—I feigned nonchalance—"just wanted to catch Kirk's interview with Saban. I figured you'd be okay without me." I was glad to see Erin smile at this.

"Even if I was okay without you, I don't want to be without you. We go together, Sock."

"You know I wouldn't miss this for the world, even for the National Championship game. This is our big championship, and it's game on. You are doing great."

"I hope so. I feel pretty good," Erin slurred a bit. "I think I like being here. It's fun. Do you think we can go back to our room after this?"

Whatever drugs they'd given her, they were obviously working. While Erin was still coherent, she certainly was woozy. In my peripheral vision, the doctors and nurses were busy at work.

"I am sure they'll let us go back to 307," I whispered in Erin's ear. "Tootie is waiting for us and rooting you on."

A doctor announced, "She's out." I knew the doctor was holding my baby, but I was too nervous to peer over the curtain.

These joyous words should ring through new parents' hearts like magic, only to be eclipsed in emotion by the unforgettable moment when the doctor places this precious bundle of life onto the mother's chest. This is how it should go. I knew that was not how it would go for us.

Time was a blur, but before I knew it, the wheels of a small cart squeaked as a nurse rolled it to us and said, "I want to introduce you to your new little girl." Erin's eyes sharpened out of the epidural haze and we both gazed at our baby Faith, the tiniest human I'd ever seen with an even tinier chest squeezing with every breath. And then she was gone, swept away by a stranger, down the raging river. Down toward an uncertain outcome. Down without her mommy or daddy to help her or rescue her.

Tears filled both our eyes as our gazes followed that cart until it was out of sight. She was born at twenty five weeks and two days and weighed one pound, fourteen ounces. Even though she was so helpless and we were supposed to be the ones protecting her, we knew that by letting her go, we were actually giving her the best chance at survival. Sometimes the most anguishing thing to do is to stay put.

I rolled up a chair and leaned my head against Erin's as we patiently waited for the completion of the procedures needed post C-section. Words were few. Which collection of letters could possibly hold the mix of emotions we were feeling?

The primary surgeon, a man with kind eyes and a dark beard, finished his sutures and stood next to us. His eyes were searching for words, deeply sorrowful.

"Your daughter is in good hands," he said. Unable to maintain eye contact, he pulled a chair close. "I know this is hard, so hard. I got into this field because I wanted to make a difference. To help young families, Moms, bring new life into this world. There's nothing like seeing a first-time mom hold her baby and whisper her love as the baby snuggles in, or the fathers beaming with pride for their baby girls and newborn sons. It's the best job in the world, and each baby makes the round-the-clock hours worth every minute of it."

His eyes lowered to the hands in his lap. "But then there are nights like tonight. Nights that test your resolve. It's just not supposed to happen this way..." Weighty moments of silence passed until he said again, "Your daughter is in good hands. Trust that we will do the best for her."

Standing, the doctor glanced down at Erin, then straight into my soul, like he knew the days ahead of us, the dark nights of despair we would face.

He reached out, placed his hand on Erin's head, then took that hand and extended it to me. As he shook my hand, he looked me in the eye as only a man can look another man in the eye. He did not say another word. He did not need to.

CHAPTER EIGHTEEN

First Impressions

The brightly lit hallway outside the NICU door was quiet. It was peaceful. And it was lonely. I stood, shifting from foot to foot, pondering what I would see on the other side of that door. It was only a few hours since Faith took her first breath; was she still alive? I'd barely glimpsed her form before. Once I walked through those doors, I would be forced to see everything about her; would she even look like a human being? Would she be in pain? I wanted to run the other way.

Erin was sleeping as comfortably as possible in 307, recovering from the long night. While I had initially crashed with her, sleep had only been my companion for a couple hours. My restlessness had led me here to the NICU; I had to know how my daughter was doing, and yet now that only a door separated me from the answer, perhaps the unknown was better. Once I knew, I could not un-know.

God, I need you, but I'm not even sure what words to pray.

My mind hacked through this forest of indecision, attempting to find a pathway of faith that would lead me out. Then, as if someone knew the condition of my heart, a prayer lifted around me. The audible words begging for peace and for the right words to pray, cut through the dense brush that covered my mind. Swiveling to see their source, it startled me to see there was no one in the hall except me. How could this be? Left without the ability to see the source of this blessing, my ears followed the gorgeous, faith-filled prayer, voiced by a woman sounding elevated in age. I half-expected to see an angel hovering over me in all her majestic glory, but instead I only saw a blank, white ceiling.

To my disappointment, there was not a celestial being, only a ceiling speaker. But then I stopped and realized what was happening. A prayer was being broadcast over the hospital loudspeaker! A prayer for faith, for peace, for safety, and wisdom for doctors, nurses, and families. Everything I would have wanted to voice to my God. The hospital was affiliated with a religious organization, so prayer wasn't completely abnormal, but what was abnormal was we had lived in this hospital for almost three weeks and had never once heard a broadcasted prayer. And I will add, we never heard this again during the rest of our stay.

I stood outside the NICU amazed. Yet again, I had experienced God's perfect timing. He had shown up in my inadequate and scared situation and handed me what I needed to take the next steps. Even if we walk through the valley of the shadows of death, He is right there beside us. I was now ready to face whatever laid on the other side of that door.

Even though more than a few people were inside the NICU, an understood expectation of quiet hung in the air. The energy felt like a cross between a library and a cemetery. Hope and dread. Life and death.

"Hello," I whispered to the attendant. "My name is Blake Hamby, and I'm here to see Faith Hamby."

"Welcome, Mr. Hamby," the sweet woman smiled as she checked her computer. "Faith is in area number five." A wave of gratitude splashed over me that her response was not an announcement of death.

"Five. Thank you. Where is that?"

"Just to your left, about twenty feet, and then you will see five."

My knees wobbled and sweat ran down my back as I followed

her directions. I had received a tour of this room during our initial stay, but now that I was actually coming to visit my baby, I noticed many more details. About a dozen preemies filled this large room, and curtains on tracks separated each area. While this would allow doctors and nurses to quickly access the babies, these areas were close quarters with no privacy for parents. What if the other parents heard me praying, or crying, or worse, singing, to my baby Faith? This setup was not at all what Dr. Carlo had described about UAB. There, each family had a private room. Again, the nagging thoughts about whether or not we should be there pattered through my mind.

At number five, I stepped into the curtained area. Our baby was in a large plastic, enclosed box with ports on either side that allowed us to access her. Faith was bigger than I had expected a preemie born at one pound, fourteen ounces to be. She also did not have as many tubes and wires as the nurses had prepared us for. Slumbering so peacefully, she looked like a tiny cherub. My heart overflowed with love, and words of thanksgiving could not help but spill out of my mouth. I would've probably started weeping had not the rustle of the curtain interrupted my first father/daughter moment with Faith.

A man wearing jeans and a Rolling Stones t-shirt stood brooding. Definitely not a nurse.

"Good morning. How are you?" I calmly but curiously asked.

First Impressions

"I was better before I saw you standing over my baby."

"What are you talking about?"

"That's my child. What are you doing and why are you in here?"

"Huh." I squinted my eyes at the man. "I thought she was mine...are you sure this is your baby?"

"Dude, look at the name right there."

Yep. That was definitely not Faith's name. The lack of privacy between baby areas just shrunk infinitely smaller. I hoped I didn't run into this guy every day.

"Well, how 'bout that," I said nervously. Not knowing what to do, I shook his hand and said, "Congratulations on the new addition to your family" and then awkwardly left.

As I retraced my steps back to the nurse's station, I found the correct number five. Pushing back the curtain, I saw Faith, truly saw her, for the first time. I lost my breath. She seemed no larger than the span of my own hand. How in the world could any human this tiny actually be living? Or have any chance to make it?

She had tubes strapped to her nose. Several wires attached to her stomach. An IV stuck into her forehead. No clothes except the tiniest of beanies. My Lord, why is this happening? This child, our child, has no chance. Several minutes of numbness passed while my heart processed what I was seeing.

Something else seemed off. What was it?

Glancing back at a few of the other preemies, then again at Faith, I realized she didn't have a normal plastic box to house her. She was surrounded by four small plexiglass walls and those were covered by a thin, plastic wrap. While most of the other babies looked like they were living inside a plastic fortress, my child was in something I would've built for my 8th grade science project. And I scored below average in 8th grade science. Just to make sure, I strode throughout the room to take a tally of the babies in the room. All had plastic fortresses, none had 8th grade science experiments. When I entered Faith's area five again, a nurse was attending to her.

"Hello, you must be Dad. My name is Sarah."

"Hey, Sarah, I was just checking out Faith."

"She's just beautiful. We've been working to make her nice and cozy."

"Really." At this, Sarah looked up at me, no doubt wondering what my cold response meant.

When I didn't offer more, she began to explain all the machines draped around Faith. There was one that measured her heart rate, one for her oxygen saturation level, and one that showed what level of oxygen she was on. As she continued with the others, my mind tried to remember all the medical lingo and purposes of each. But there was really only one question on my mind.

"So, why isn't Faith in one of those strong box things?"

"Strong...box...things?" Sarah was confused.

"Yeah, like that one right there," I pointed at the box Rolling Stones guys's baby was in. "All the other preemies have one. Why doesn't Faith have one of those?"

"Oh, what she has is perfectly fine," Sarah said matter-of-factly. "This type is how preemies have been kept for years."

"Okay. If this is perfectly fine, then why did you change to the other box?"

"Well, that other box, or incubator, does have some additional benefits. But this one is just as good, or, it is fine. It will be good."

I was not convinced. "Tell me about these additional benefits? What are those?"

Sarah was getting uncomfortable. Good. Faith was probably uncomfortable laying naked under a canopy of Saran wrap. She responded, "I don't know. It just, you know, that newer type of incubator keeps the baby warm. And maybe it's better for the environment. And other things, I guess."

"Better for the environment? What does that mean? How is it better for the environment?"

"Well, because it does not have to use the Saran wrap on top, so we are wasting less materials."

Aha! I was right! That was just basic Saran wrap, the same flimsy stuff I had in my kitchen. I bet UAB didn't use Saran wrap.

"I love the environment. And I love my baby. So how about we get us one of those new incubators? My wife and I, we recycle, you know. We would like to help with that."

Sarah looked embarrassed. "I'm sorry, Mr. Hamby. That's not possible right now."

"And why is that?"

"We, uh, we, well, we don't have any left. They are all being used by other children. It has been busy."

I just stared at her with a long "are you kidding me?" look. At some point Sarah became uncomfortable with my blank stare, dropped her eyes, and on her way out said the doctor would be in soon, and I could talk to him about it.

Walking back to 307, I resolved that our baby would have a box. Even if we had to buy it, she would have a box.

CHAPTER NINETEEN

Saran Wrap

Day Two of Faith's life brought with it three monumental events in our lives. First, our church started our annual 21 Days of Prayer and Fasting. Second, Erin was going to go see her second-born child for the first time. And third, we got to cap off the day with friends coming to our hospital room to watch the Alabama vs. LSU National Championship game. I was thankful we had sandwiched Erin's journey to meet Faith between these two other joyful events. I needed all the help I could find to offset my concern about how

Erin would handle gazing at her fragile child, locked in an 8th grade science experiment.

Wheeling Erin into the NICU was surreal, like we were living someone else's life. Adding to the strangeness was Erin's insistence that we not stop to talk to anyone we passed along the way: the nurses, the doctors, other parents, or even the attendant at the front desk. Under normal circumstances, Erin's random conversations would take at least twenty minutes upon entry and thirty during exit.

Pushing Erin up to the side of Faith's poorly formed science experiment box, I steadied myself to handle her reaction to our daughter receiving subpar care. Either her Cajun lioness within would erupt, and I'd need to help put out the fires, or her mommy heart would break, and I'd need to console and love her through her tears. Apparently, I'd misjudged my wife. Instead of anger or sorrow, Erin's eyes brightened, and an unspoken radiance poured out of her. Gazing at Faith laying between four plexiglass walls draped in common Saran wrap with wires and needles protruding from almost every part of her tiny body, Erin saw what I did not see. She saw birthday parties. Movie nights by the fire. Camping trips. Scraped knees. First days of school. Snuggling on the couch after her first heartbreak. Celebrating her glowing smile after the smelly boy she brought home finally popped the question. Erin saw the girl growing into a woman. The women she had risked her life for.

What she saw, that I did not, was hope. My wife saw the very hand of God sitting twelve inches in front of her.

"She is so beautiful, Sock," she whispered. "And so tiny." Her trembling hand reached her mouth as she silently expressed her wonder and awe. After several moments, she added, "We are looking at a miracle right now. Of science. Of medicine. Do you realize if she had been born even just a few decades ago, there would be almost no chance she would live?" She shook her head in disbelief.

"God is so, so good to us, Sock," she continued. "Faith should still be inside my womb, being knit together by Him, but here she is right before our eyes! And alive! God is giving us a glimpse into life being created." Tears streamed down her cheeks.

"Thank you, Erin," I said through a tight throat as I held back my own tears.

"For what, Sock?"

"For helping me see what I would never see without you."

After our hearts were full with thankfulness for our baby, and a few badly sung lullabies from Erin, I rolled my wife's wheelchair back to 307. With this chapter of our day safely behind us, I was excited to detach from reality for a little while and get lost in the National Championship game. But before we could welcome our friends and let Kirk and Chris guide us through the grudge match that was sure to unfold, we had another visitor to entertain.

One of the neonatologists Dr. Armand paid us a visit. Maybe it was a defense mechanism to not have the conversation go the route of our last one with "Dr. Happy," maybe it was my desire to get to watching the game, maybe it was a bit of both, but as soon as the obligatory small chat was over, I was ready with my questions.

Me: How long do you think we will be here?

Dr. A: We like to target a few weeks after your due date.

Me: Once Erin is released, how often can we come and see Faith?

Dr. A: As much as you want, you just won't be able to spend the night.

Me: What are the most common, immediate issues for preemies like Faith?

Dr. A: Well, as you might imagine, there are many. Some of the main things we are monitoring right now are brain bleeds, how her stomach is digesting food, how well she is able to breathe along with her oxygen levels, and also doing our best to ensure she does not get sick with something as simple as a cold or flu.

Me: Something tells me I don't want to know this, but I have to ask...what is a brain bleed?

Dr. A: I realize the term sounds very scary. Preemies, especially ones under three pounds, have tiny and very fragile blood vessels in their brains, and these can hemorrhage. In most instances, the bleeds are minor, and the baby's body simply absorbs the fluid.

I liked this guy. He matched my pace and cut straight to the chase.

Me: Okay, well, we will believe that will be the case for Faith. Our last conversation with a neonatologist was incredibly difficult...so many long-term effects. What are we really in danger of?

Dr. A: I try to encourage my parents instead of worrying about all the 'what ifs' that could happen down the road. It's best to focus on the things that are right in front of us.

Erin piped in: Thank you, Dr. Armando. I agree with that completely.

Dr. Armando sat down on a stool and looked back and forth between us. "I can only imagine the last several weeks you both have had and this, right here, is not the outcome you were hoping for. I need you to know that NICU stays are roller coasters; Faith will have good days followed by really bad days. The path won't always be clear, and sometimes the steps you've taken forward can be erased very quickly. But after doing this for many years, the parents that handle it the best are those who are united in their resolve to find joy in each day together, no matter what that day might bring. I wish I could tell you this was going to be easy, but I can't. It is not. But you have my word that we are going to do the very best we can for your child."

The gravity of his words weighted the air in the room.

"We appreciate that more than you know, Dr. Armando," Erin said.

"We really do," I added. "And that does lead me to one of my last questions. What is the deal with the science experiment that Faith is being housed in?" I ignored that Erin looked at me like I was talking French.

"I'm sorry?" the doctor asked. "I don't understand what you mean."

"The Saran wrap contraption you have her in. Why doesn't she have a fancy box like the other babies?"

"Oh, yes," he smiled. "Nurse Sarah said you were curious about the incubator."

"I'm more than a little curious."

"We are out of those at the moment."

"How can you be out? That seems really hard to imagine. Isn't taking care of preemies what you do? My baby needs that. Don't you agree she is very vulnerable to sickness?"

"Yes, I would agree but I can assure you what she is in is fine. This is how we have taken care of preemies for years."

"Yeah, I get that, and Nurse Sarah said the same thing, but the mortality rates were not so great historically, either. Obviously those box incubators are better or else you would not have every other baby in them."

Dr. Armando took too long to answer before I dropped my big idea. "That being the case, we would like to buy one."

Now both my wife and the doctor were looking at me like I was speaking French.

"We would like to buy one for our baby. We don't want to take one from someone else, but we are willing to buy a new one for Faith, and then y'all can keep it after we leave. How quickly do you think you can get one here?"

"Mr. Hamby, we could get one here fairly quickly, but I don't think you understand what you are offering. They're not cheap."

"I understand they are expensive, but we want what is best for our daughter and money should not stand in the way of that. So how much will this set us back? $5k? $10k? We are willing to pay that."

"Mr. Hamby, I can see that you are a caring father, a passionate person, and I appreciate you wanting to provide the best for your daughter, but I can assure you she is fine in the setup she has."

"I really don't want 'fine.' I want the best there is to offer, so I want to buy her an incubator. What's the damage? $10k?"

"Higher."

"$20k?" His silence pushed me up. "$30k?"

"Like I said, these incubators are not cheap."

Sheepishly I asked, "$35k?"

Dr. Armando's eyes were compassionate when he said, "They usually run around $38k each, and then some, depending on how many options the hospital wants."

The heat of frustration bubbled inside me. Why is this happening? Our child is barely alive as it is and now we had to settle for some half-rate, old school contraption to keep her warm and shield her from whatever illness can walk into the NICU.

Yielding to my better judgment, I let these thoughts exist only in my mind. Erin continued to lead our conversation, and Dr. Armando was very gracious as he continued to assure us that Faith was in the best place she could be. Erin was eager to express her agreement.

I couldn't get on the bandwagon. In fact, the images that continued to run through my mind were the private rooms at the NICU in UAB where they had boxes for everyone.

CHAPTER TWENTY

National Champions

The Alabama game that evening was a good distraction. With our room packed with several of our friends, and a few nurses to boot, it felt like a true party. Erin was feeling better by the minute, no lingering placenta issues remained, and Faith was as stable as could be expected. While joy and thankfulness filled me, guilt niggled the back of my mind. Was it right to have fun while my tiny baby was fighting for her every breath down the hall? Granted, there was absolutely nothing I could do to help her, save sitting next to her box and staring at her. But as a Daddy I had a need to care for her.

The cheers of my friends lifted us up, and there was plenty of reason for celebration. Alabama handled LSU with a 21-0 victory, shutting out the Tigers and only allowing them to cross the 50-yard line once the entire game. It was brutal for LSU, and it felt fantastic to be on the winning side of something, even if it was a silly football game that I had no part in.

After everyone left, I went to see Faith. As I walked through the dark hallways of the hospital, I imagined this is what those LSU players must've felt like as they exited the field and passed through the dark tunnels toward their locker rooms. When I arrived at Faith's side, I found all I wanted to do was pick her up and cradle her in my arms. I wanted to hold her so tight that nothing harmful could penetrate my grip. Feeling that if I gazed too long, I might actually rip off the Saran wrap and pick her up. I pulled out my journal and wrote.

> Alabama played LSU for the National Championship tonight. We won 21-0. While I was on the winning side tonight for the game, I think I can relate more with the Tigers these last several months of my life. Ever since the first night Erin woke up bleeding, I wonder if I have scored any points in the arena of faith? Have I even made it past the 50-yard line? No matter what type of faithful offense I have tried to establish, there is an opponent fighting me, keeping me from even getting

to midfield. Sure, I have had moments when I've caught the ball of faith, but no sooner have I grasped it than a vicious, unrelenting opponent tackles me.

Lord, I wonder if You are proud of how I am playing this game? I feel like I am doing pretty good at 'faking it 'til I make it' to the people around me, but You know my struggles. You know my innermost thought. Are You disappointed in me? Am I enough in Your eyes? While I get the feeling these are not the right questions, I still can't help feeling like You're standing on the sidelines, watching my true feelings play out on the playing field of my heart, and You are as disappointed as the LSU fans were tonight that I just can't get my act together.

My mind seems incapable of escaping the tight grip of the reality of just how fragile Faith really is. I am smart enough to understand that our journey ahead is uncertain and a low probability that Faith will come through this without serious issues, if she comes through it at all.

In my heart of hearts, I trust You, Lord, and know that You are here with us, and I honestly don't even struggle with why this is happening, although I do wonder why this happened when it did. But I guess what I struggle with the most is purpose. What is the purpose of all of this? Why can I not seem to find the resolve inside my heart to see the bigger picture? I am willing to walk through the valley of the shadow of death, no matter what that valley holds, but I want to know that it matters. I want to know the journey is worth it. I need to know there is purpose in all the pain. In short, I need to see a purpose bigger than what is right in front of me because what is right in front of me looks fairly pointless.

With that, I closed my journal. Staring at Faith's delicate body, with the beeps and chirps of the monitors surrounding me, I prayed that the Lord would protect and heal Faith, that He would somehow use all this to make a difference, and that He would show me His purpose for this pain.

But still, the answers to my questions remained as elusive to me as the fifty-yard line was to LSU.

CHAPTER TWENTY-ONE

Mama Elephants

"Elephant Moms are some of the fiercest on the planet." Rolling over in her hands a stuffed University of Alabama mascot that her dad had brought back from the championship game, Erin seemed a million miles away.

"It was really nice of your dad to buy that for us at the game last night," I said of the fuzzy elephant with a red "A" stitched on its belly. "And it sure was nice of your dad to catch the early flight out of New Orleans to come see us. I am sure the loss by LSU and the generous number of cocktails were not a recipe for an easy morning."

"They will ferociously defend and fight for their babies, to the death." This completely random comment from Erin made me realize she hadn't heard a word I just said. "Not that long ago, I was watching a National Geographic show that talked about how the elephant moms guard their calves like a fortress. They put the babies in the middle of the herd, and the moms never leave their side."

Was she crying? At the angle we were sitting, I couldn't quite see her face. She must've felt my eyes searching because she shifted farther from my sightline. She most definitely was crying.

"It was fascinating," she continued. "And I never knew this before. They truly mourn the deaths of their babies; they even instinctively do a burial ritual with the rest of the herd. Scientists have recorded elephant families coming back to these places of burial over and over throughout the years to pace around their burial place."

I wasn't sure why we were talking about elephants, but I tried to be considerate of Erin's feelings and simply said, "I had no idea."

And then I got it.

Tonight was our last night at the hospital; tomorrow morning the doctors would discharge us, and we would return home. Without Faith.

My chest tightened, and my eyes burned.

"Erin," my throat choked with emotion, and I had to pause before I could speak. "Erin, I'm so sorry. I would do anything in my power to not leave Faith here."

My beautiful wife turned her tear-stained face toward me, and my heart broke into a million pieces. In her eyes was a primal fire, burning and swirling with grief, anger, helplessness, and strength. All these emotions shone through her gaze simultaneously, and I wondered how her fragile body could contain them. But I also had my own internal inferno brewing.

As a father, every ounce of me yearned to protect and fight for my baby girl. Ill-equipped to do either for our twenty-five-week-old preemie, I was forced to abdicate that responsibility to nurses and doctors I had just met. My gut felt ripped open in the passivity of that choice. How would I know they were watching her every minute of the day? Would they love her enough? Care for her enough? What if something went terribly wrong...would they be there in time to save my girl? There was no way to know without a shadow of a doubt, and that uncertainty devoured my peace of mind.

However, I was also a husband, and right now my wife needed me to help her, to come alongside, take her hand, and walk with her through the extreme difficulty of leaving behind her new baby who was fighting for her life. Gathering Erin in my arms, she melted into my chest, and together we sobbed.

I'm not sure how long we held each other, but when we both settled and were breathing quietly, I found my voice. "Father, we need You right now. Give us the courage to walk into this next season with our baby girl. Help us trust that You love her and care for her more than we do; that she was Yours before she ever was ours. Give Erin and me peace to know Your hand will protect Faith, will cradle Faith, as we have to live apart from her, and until we can hold her ourselves. You are good, God, and You've been so good to us every step of the way. Heal Faith and give us your peace, in Jesus's name."

"Amen, and amen," Gloria's soft, rich voice closed out my prayer. When Erin saw Gloria, fresh tears flowed.

"Miss Gloria," I said as I pulled in Erin tighter. "This is our last night."

"Miss Gloria," Erin whispered through her sobs, "you have meant so very much to me. I'm going to miss seeing you every afternoon."

Gloria left her cleaning cart, sat next to Erin, and took her hand.

"Now you look at me, Sugar." She waited until she had locked eyes with Erin's. "Your baby Faith is gonna be just fine. You need to believe that God knew. He knew way before you did, and He already has put inside you all the strength you need to walk this out. You got a good husband and a good God. You watch and see...won't He do it."

"How am I going to leave her?" Erin choked on the words.

"The best place she could be is in the hands of her God, and He don't sleep, and He don't slumber. He's gonna be watchin' over her every minute of the day. And your love stretches from where you are to wherever your baby girl is. Do you believe that?"

Miss Gloria didn't break eye contact until she got an answer from Erin.

"Yes, ma'am," Erin said. "I do. I really do believe that."

"Then you're gonna be all right." Then she looked straight into my soul. "You both are gonna be just fine. All you gotta do is trust. Trusting is easy when everything is good. Real trust, real faith, comes when things ain't so certain."

With a squeeze of Erin's hand, Gloria transitioned from her true purpose to resume her official job. We listened to her calming voice as she hummed through her chores. After Gloria finished cleaning, she prayed for us. Erin gave Gloria a long hug before she left, thanking her for so much more than keeping our room spotless in every way.

In silence we readied ourselves for our final night in 307. If home was where your heart was, then as long as Faith was living under her Saran wrapped box here in this hospital, we now had two homes. One home with Rebekah, and one home here with

Faith.

I scooted my couch bed as close to Erin's as possible so I could hold her hand until she fell asleep.

CHAPTER TWENTY-TWO
Caring Bridge

At night when my dream-state mind traveled back to my boyhood, my grandmother's farmhouse was a location that often popped up. One day, several months before Faith was born, after a business meeting, I found myself in the area and decided to check on my grandmother's property. My grandmother had moved away and no one in the family really visited anymore, so I was curious what condition I would find it in after sitting empty for years. As I passed by the property, I was shocked to find the house was missing. Had someone stolen it? Is it even possible to steal a house? Had it been so long I'd forgotten where it was? Certainly not.

Parking my truck close to where I thought I had parked that U-Haul years ago—back when Bardwell had helped me move my stuff there for storage—I decided to walk the property. Ahead, where her house should've been, was a small forest of trees and shrubs. The closer I got, I realized I had not forgotten at all. I was just unable to see the house. Those trees and shrubs, unchecked by normal care, had successfully cocooned her entire house! It wasn't until I was right on it I could see the entrance to the porch.

Even though Erin and I had only been home from the hospital for a couple of days, our lives reminded me of that farmhouse. The perpetual noise and responsibilities of life were creeping around us, and the peace and simplicity of what we had experienced in Room 307 already seemed like a distant memory. Not until our return to this busy-ness and demand did I realize that life had actually given Erin and me a timeout. Now life required us to hop back into action on the playing field.

Erin's body had not fully recovered from the caesarean birth, so she was rightly not up to shouldering much. Meanwhile a mound of work greeted me at the office, Rebekah desired and deserved attention, and all the normality's of life, like cleaning, cooking, eating, and showering, commanded more time than I cared to give them. Because there was Faith, and that most important necessity loomed over both Erin and me like the farmhouse's trees.

While we felt helpless to physically help her, we would visit her at least twice a day at the NICU. In those short two days, we had already learned the rhythm of the NICU. It was a cycle of hearing the updates from the nurses, watching her monitors in our squished area number five, staring at her, praying for her, and occasionally singing poorly over her. While those efforts were well and good, they all seemed so inadequate. Our love for Faith burned inside and compelled us to do more, to pray harder, to ask better questions, and to research more. I felt as if I was my grandmother's house, enshrouded by trees of helplessness and shrubberies of the thorny unknowns. The shadows closed in and I doubted I had what it would take to survive for another four months. Impossible.

But we still did what we could. As such, after work, I'd gone to visit Faith. My frustrations and burdens had tormented my mind all day. Now it was late at night, and I was beyond tired from trying to fight through the trees. Alone in my truck as I drove home, I realized I'd been so preoccupied with the tasks of the day I hadn't eaten lunch. The lights of many fast-food restaurants lined my route, but I couldn't bring myself to turn in. Eating heavy, fried food would only make my physical body feel as disgusting as my emotional body felt. I would rather just feel empty.

Pulling into my driveway, I realized Rebekah would be asleep, and I had not seen her all day. Erin would also be asleep. She had been through so much, I didn't want to wake her. The last two nights, at home in our bedroom together, had seemed empty. It was like we were an incomplete family without Faith with us. Being together felt disjointed and sad.

My emotional and mental fatigue cloaked me like a weighted blanket as I quietly crossed the threshold of our humble Homewood, Alabama, home. The unlit Christmas tree lurking in the corner drooped with the same heaviness I felt in my heart. So much promise had accompanied its festive arrival into our home, but now, weeks after the close of Christmas, that tree stood dark and lifeless. I longed for the normal life the ornaments represented. But our normal had evaporated, just like the life that had once held the tree in perfect form.

Walking down the only hallway in our 1,100 square foot home, I stopped at the door to peek into our one-and-a-half-year-old daughter, Rebekah's, room. Erin and I had planned on graduating our first born out of this room so Faith could take over the small space. That thought felt as sad as the dead Christmas tree in our den looked. Staring into Rebekah's room, I noticed her baby picture framed in silver above her crib. Erin's Mom had taken it on the day Erin and I brought Rebekah home from the hospital after her birth. That occasion had been filled with such excitement and hope. Thinking about the birth of Faith felt like I was a part of a bad magic trick where anxiety and despair replaced the excitement and hope.

Leaving Rebekah's room, I realized I should not wake Erin so I collapsed onto the bed in our guest room, still clutching my briefcase.

Pulling my laptop from the briefcase, I let my eyes adjust to the bright screen, half hoping the light would break through the gloom in my mind. But when I tried to focus on my clients' medical insurance, my mother-in-law's voice surfaced instead: "Blake, why don't you start a CaringBridge site? Let people know what's happening?"

I had dismissed that idea as quickly as she'd offered it. "Who has the time to read those emails?" I'd argued. When sent to me, I'd keep them in my inbox, fully intending to read them, but then after a month or so, I'd usually end up deleting them with a mild level of guilt. Wouldn't it be better to just save my friends the guilt?

Trying to turn my attention back to the spreadsheet outlining the medical insurance that was supposed to protect strangers, I wondered if the person who designed our medical coverage knew the one hospital my family needed was out-of-network. Which, I now had first-hand knowledge that out-of-network was just a code word for personal bankruptcy. I lingered on that thought long enough to realize wasting time on a CaringBridge site was a better alternative.

The CaringBridge landing page presented a "Start a Site" button, which I clicked and easily followed the first several prompts. My fingers froze when the final prompt read, "Tell Us Your Story."

How do I answer that? What was our story?

The story of our last several months, culminating in the last few days, was not one I'd ever wanted to call ours. It was certainly not the story I had been praying for. A story that was built on phrases like "your baby has a zero percent chance of surviving" and "we cannot save both of you." This story had arrived uninvited and proceeded to twist our lives into something I barely recognized.

Sitting there, I contemplated everything and nothing at the same time. Stuck in my bed of indecision, I reached back into my briefcase and pulled out my journal. Thumbing through the entries of the last several months, I shuttered at the thought of letting everyone see my real emotions. Why would I do that? I didn't even have a Facebook page. I preferred to let my emotions pour out on a page only I can see.

But in disregard for my better judgement, I clicked on the first line under "Tell Us Your Story." Closing my eyes, I surrendered, and the words flowed from me, onto the keys, and out on the page. As I wrote, the words were not what I expected. They felt like words coming from someone else's voice. A voice I would get to know well.

Hello World, my name is Faith. My mom and dad tell me I came a little early, but the Lord told me I was perfect in every way and I arrived right on time. He also told me that my mom has a tendency to run a bit late so my being early might be a good balance. I hope you enjoy reading my story.

The interesting thing about my story is it is still being written. I have no idea where it is going to take us, but I guess that is how it is with a great story. You know the ones. Those that keep you up late into the night because you have to find out what happens next. Page turners. That's the kind of story I want to be a part of.

But the most exciting thing about my story is that I get to go through it with each of you. It will be like the adventures of old. We can pretend to be Huck Finn and Tom Sawyer, sailing down the mighty Mississippi with danger around every bend. Our we can pretend we are Shackleton and his men, braving the cold and lonesome icebergs, fighting to make it to safety and a warm bed.

It's funny, but that's kind of what it is like here in the NICU. Me and all my friends in here are surrounded by some things that seem pretty scary. And come to think of it, our path down the river of life in front of us looks pretty bumpy, full of twists and turns. But as scary and lonely as it can seem, it's better knowing that we are in this together. So thanks for reading, and be sure to check back for the next pages of our grand adventure!

P.S. Thanks for praying for me. You don't know how much difference that makes for me and my family.

By now I had nestled deeply into the bed, and reading what I had just written brought a smile to my face. Something familiar lit my heart and pushed back some of the emptiness. It was that same feeling I had when I wrote my secret thoughts in my journal. Only this time, my secrets were not so secret.

Not sure how people would react to the whimsical way I'd chosen to tell our story, I decided to just go with it. Hitting save and post, I wondered if anyone would read it.

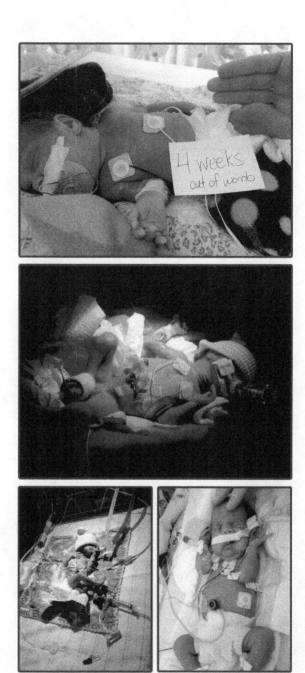

Faith in NICU

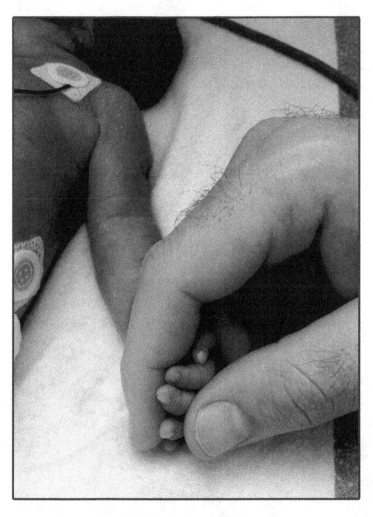
Faith holding her dad's hand

Blake holding his daughter, Faith

Erin and her daughter, Faith

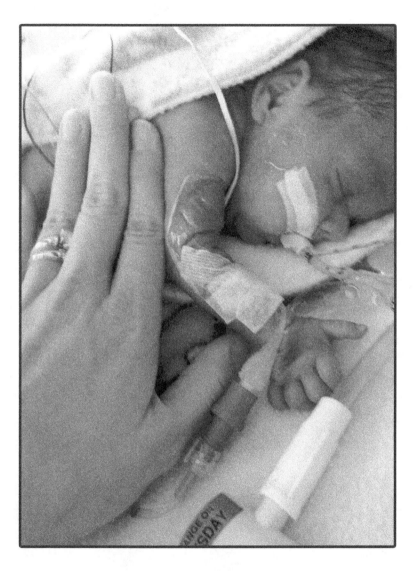

Erin's hand and her daughter, Faith

CHAPTER TWENTY-THREE

Good Trouble

"You guys are never going to believe what just happened!"

The whirlwind that was Erin's mom touched down and blew through our front door. "Ami Ami" to our girls, and "Ms. Pam" to me, she never ceased to add excitement to our lives, which I enjoyed most of the time. But this morning I was still waiting for my coffee to kick in.

I'm fairly certain Ms. Pam met a stranger once when she first went to college in 1972, but since then she'd given up the idea that there is such a thing as a stranger. Growing up in South Louisiana and a proud Cajun, she holds a few firm beliefs: (1) The only acceptable place to be on a Spring Friday night is eating boiled crawfish; (2) Fall Saturdays are reserved for LSU football; (3) Winter brings with it the most treasured national holiday, Mardi Gras; (4) Summer brings so much heat and humidity, with insects the size of flying mice, that one questions why any sane person would live there.

"Blake, you have to watch this video." Ms. Pam was breathless as she dropped her purse, almost bigger than her slight frame, on the counter, essential oils and vitamin bottles spilling and rolling about. She had offered to stay with us for a couple of days to help while I was at work. She had actually driven through the night to be here first thing this morning and apparently left her home in such a rush, she'd packed her entire organic medicine cabinet in her purse. "I have never in my life experienced anything so awesome."

Plopping down on the sofa, she patted the cushion next to her. "Where's Erin and Rebekah?"

"Erin's finishing up in the shower and Rebekah is still asleep." I chugged my hot coffee, ignoring the burn.

"I'll show them later. I can't wait." She slapped the cushion harder. "Get over here!"

As I sat down, she continued. "This just happened when I was leaving Target this morning."

"How early does Target open? Why did you go there after driving all night?" I asked as the video displayed a shot from the driver's perspective inside her moving car, steering wheel in the background, and something weird in her palm. "What is—"

"A hummingbird. Blake, that's a hummingbird in my hand!"

"How are you driving your car if your phone is in one hand and a bird is in the other?"

"A hummingbird, Blake. That's a real hummingbird!" She obviously was not going to address my insinuation of her reckless driving. "As I was leaving the store, I saw him on the sidewalk. He looked wounded, and I couldn't just leave him there. Who would do that?"

Me. I would do that. After at least thirty seconds, I couldn't help myself. "Ms. Pam...how are you driving your car if you—"

"Shhhh...wait for it..."

The bird launched off her hand and started zinging around inside her car! The buzz from his wings lifted over Ms. Pam's ecstatic narration on the video: "Oh my!! Look at that! Oh, thank the Lord, he is healed!" (The phone camera darted around as she attempted to keep up with this tiny bird's lightning pace.) "This is a miracle. I can't believe I'm seeing this right now. What am I going to do with him now? How do I keep a hummingbird as a pet? Look at him go! I wish I still had the Bird Lady's number who helped me when I had my hawk." With that, the screen went dark.

As I held the dark phone in my hand, I stared at the blank screen. I could feel the pull of Ms. Pam's expectation for my response. So many questions were darting around my head, rather like that bird in her car.

"Ms. Pam..." I smiled.

"I know!" She giggled with wonder in her eyes. "Can you believe you just saw that?"

"You are correct. I cannot believe I just saw that. In fact, there are so many things about that video I cannot believe."

"He just, boom, came alive and started flying, right before my eyes."

"Who is the Bird Lady?"

"It was a miracle, Blake, an honest to goodness miracle."

"You had a hawk?"

"Hey, baby girl!" Ms. Pam chimed as Erin entered the room. "You have to see this video! I witnessed a miracle today, right in my own car!"

"Hey, Mama!" Erin hugged and kissed her mom. "Thank you so much for coming. You can't know how much we appreciate it. Rebekah is still waking up, and Blake and I really want to get to the NICU to see Faith this morning. You and I will go back again after dinner, okay?"

"Of course, honey!" Ms. Pam answered.

"Are you ready, Sock?" Erin asked me.

"Yep. Ms. Pam, help yourself to whatever you want to eat."

"Oh, I was thinking about taking Rebekah out for breakfast," Ms. Pam said.

"No!" I abruptly answered, which garnered a rude look from Erin. "I mean..." I fished out cash from my wallet and wrote a phone number on a sticky note. "I promised Rebekah last night that you'd order her favorite donuts from this great bakery. And guess what? It delivers!" I had to do everything in my power to prevent Ms. Pam from getting behind the wheel with my little girl in her car...ever.

"That'll be fun," Pam chirped. "Can I go see if she's awake?"

"Of course, Mama. She's excited to see you."

As we were driving to the hospital, Erin asked, "Why did you sleep in the guest room last night?"

I glanced over to see if Erin's face appeared hurt or angry. "I got home late, knew I was going to toss and turn, and didn't want to wake you up."

"Sock, we sleep together. Don't do that again."

"I love you," I smiled. "Hey, have you ever heard of CaringBridge?"

"That one where people blog about hospital stays and such?"

"Yeah. I think I started us a site last night."

"That sounds cool."

I hoped Erin's underwhelming response was not indicative of how others would respond to what I'd posted last night.

At the hospital, the nurses greeted us with good news. Faith's oxygen levels were holding strong, she was feeding well through her tubes, and she showed no signs of intestinal issues. While all these conversations about our baby were surreal, the fact that our tiny girl was alive and progressing well lifted our spirits.

Erin yearned to connect physically with Faith, so the nurses allowed her to rest her hand on Faith's bare back. If this was the only skin-to-skin contact allowed, Erin would take every second. As her seemingly enormous hand blanketed our preemie, we marveled through tears and whispers at the awesome sight of God's delicate creation.

Hours later, Erin and I walked into our home a little taller, a little lighter, and infinitely more grateful that our God was working on our behalf. Later that night, after a gumbo dinner courtesy of Ms. Pam, the four of us crowded into Rebekah's room and played dolls until our baby girl started falling asleep. Lavishing attention on our daughter was another blessing, as the circumstances of the last few months had jostled her schedule around. As we laughed in her room, there was an odd sense of incompletion. Ms. Pam sensed it, too, because as soon as Rebekah was sleeping, she brought up Erin's offer from earlier in the day to go visit Faith in the NICU, even though she was not supposed to be allowed in.

Exhausted, I tucked myself into bed and opened the computer to check if anyone had read and responded to our new Caring-Bridge post. My eyes popped wide when I saw all the comments. I never imagined how good their acknowledgments would make me feel. I figured it was only right to respond to them, since they'd taken time out of their days to comment and pray. Clicking on the post link, I felt the words tumble out of my fingers as if they had been there all along, waiting for the right moment to be released.

To my surprise, the words that flowed stemmed not from my own thoughts, but somehow from Faith's. Sharing the world through how I thought Faith might see it, felt like it was drawing me closer to her.

> Today, I'm a fiver! It's my fifth day of life on earth, outside my mommy's belly. And I have to say, I'm killing this thing called life. I've had a lot of firsts, which, since I'm new, is probably not that uncommon, but it's so much fun!
> One, the nurses fed me my mommy's milk and my belly did great with it. Two, I breathed well enough today that I got to have oxygen through a soft thing in my nose rather than something called a C-pap that is kind of like a garbage can attached to my face. And let me tell you, that is so. Much. Better. Three, I got to feel my mommy's warm hand on my back, and it was the most wonderful feeling in the world. I heard the doctors tell

Mommy and Daddy that their touch will help me grow strong, and it really does make me feel like I can take on the world. To try my best to remember to breathe. And I love hearing my parents' voices because the happy sound is so much clearer than when I was inside my mommy's tummy. Their voices make me feel safe. And loved. Except when they sing. But don't tell them I said so. By the way, did you notice I can already count to three? I was pretty proud of that.

Oh! I also got to meet Ami Ami tonight. I don't think she was supposed to be in here with my mommy, but something tells me she doesn't get too worried about the rules in life that seem a little silly to her. Plus, she kept showing the nurses a funny video that had something to do with a bird, so the nurses really loved Ami Ami.

Speaking of love, my tiny heart is bursting with the love from you. That you read my first post and even left comments lets me know I am not alone, and I am so thankful for that.

As you know, I am not very old, and I don't know much about how the world works, but one thing I am learning is how wonderful it is to have buddies. Buddies like you who will speak for me when I cannot speak for myself. Or buddies like Ami Ami who was so driven by her love for me that she didn't let some little rule stand in her way of seeing me. As I said, I don't know a lot, but I know how good these things make me feel.

My dad told me about a man named Mr. John. I think his last name was Lewis. Anyway, he has worked his whole life to help people and would talk about getting into a little "Good Trouble." My dad also told me about some buddies a long time ago who had a friend who could not walk, and they wanted this man to see another man named Mr. Jesus because He could heal their friend. Well, they could not get into the house where this Mr. Jesus was, so they got themselves up on the roof and cut one big hole in it and lowered their buddy down to Mr. Jesus. And Mr. Jesus healed the friend. I guess that is Good Trouble.

Okay, I am going to snuggle in and get some rest now. As I do, I will pray that you will have buddies like my Ami Ami or Mr. John or those roof cutting guys. Buddies that love you enough to not be afraid of getting into a little Good Trouble to help make this big old world a better place.

> *"But they could not find a way to take him in because of so many people. They made a hole in the roof over where Jesus stood. Then they let the bed with the sick man on it down before Jesus. When Jesus saw their faith, He said to the man, 'Friend, your sins are forgiven.'"*
> Luke 5:19–20, NLV

As I read back over what I had written, I wondered if people would think it was cute or corny? Either way, it just felt right to me. But even if it felt right and drew me closer to Faith, I questioned why I would write from Faith's perspective. Maybe it was because I didn't want to deal with the situation directly. Or because my personality gets uncomfortable in serious situations and resorts to jokes or sarcasm. Or maybe it was simply a way to communicate Faith's issues in a non-boring, non-medical way. It was probably all of these.

But I think more than anything, it just felt wonderful to give my daughter, Faith, a voice.

CHAPTER TWENTY-FOUR

Round and Round

The mall's brightly colored indoor carousel was Rebekah's delight. When she and Erin passed by as I sat on the observer's bench, she'd giggle as I waved and made goofy faces. Each time I'd try to contort my face into an expression she hadn't seen before. While Rebekah loved the game, I'm pretty sure Erin was thinking how hard it would be to unsee my ugly faces. I might have been blowing my chances for any romance later that night.

Once the game grew old for my toddler, I relaxed on the

bench and simply watched the movement and rhythm of the carousel. Up and down. Round and round. The same song over and over. Because the mall was unpopulated at this time of the day, the ride worker was giving extra-long rides for the kids. Up and down. Round and round.

Our family's new normal was much the same. Since coming home from the hospital, what at first seemed hectic had already morphed into a rhythm. Funny how fast we can adapt, even with terrible situations. Erin and I would wake up, pray Psalm 91 together, and since our church was still in their annual observation of 21 Days of Prayer and Fasting, many mornings one of us would attend the early morning prayer meetings. Then I'd stop by the hospital on my way to work, Erin would visit during the day, then I'd come home, eat dinner, play with Rebekah, and both Erin and I would visit Faith while Ms. Pam put Rebekah to bed. Then we'd come home and Ms. Pam would distract us with stories about who knows what before we called the NICU one last time to get a report, then collapse into bed, emotionally and physically spent. Round and round. Round and round.

One unexpected blessing in this rhythm was CaringBridge. That was a horse that always seemed to be up as it circled around each night, carrying a load of encouragement I hadn't expected. More and more friends engaged with the blogs told from Faith's perspective, leaving us encouraging messages and beautifully written prayers. The last few nights, Erin and I would start reading the posts out loud and end up holding each other on the couch, crying like we had just finished watching Jack sink away from Rose in the movie Titanic.

Sitting in the mall, I grinned from ear to ear as I reflected on the CaringBridge site. I must've appeared strange because Erin giggled at me as her horse rotated by. Self-conscious, I attempted my best poker face as my attention returned to the horses, wondering who'd designed each of these horses. Every single one of them was different and decorated in an over-the-top fashion. One horse was actually an enormous cat, while another appeared to be some ostrich horse blend. Starting at the horses, I realized they were a picture of our new life with Faith. If the circling motion was our schedule, the constant up and down of the varied horse creatures was the reality for Faith. Each day had a semblance of something I recognized, but there was also some new and strange twist blended in to catch us off guard.

In the mornings when I would visit, sometimes Faith would be doing well. Her breathing strong, her body at peace. By the time Erin and I went back in the evening, we might find her stable, or we might find that she had plummeted, her vitals popping around at terrible numbers.

As I watched all the various horses circling on the carousel, I thought about how each up-and-down horse presented a different life-threating issue. Maybe the ostrich horse was the threat of brain bleeds, the cat horse could be Faith's inability to digest Erin's milk, the closely related dog horse was the never-ending threat of deadly infection. But there was one horse carousel workers did not put on kid carousels. It was a dark horse that always stayed low and pulled the air out of your lungs if you dared to look too closely at it. That was Faith's breathing.

In just the week since I'd become a NICU Dad, I'd learned more than I'd ever wanted to know about the countless medical issues that can target a human body, particularly a frail, premature human body. Many of the most serious issues for a preemie are related to the lungs. Because Faith's lungs had not had time to develop fully, they were still not yet ready to breathe air. They needed time to mature enough to do their work. Her intake of oxygen should normally be around 21%, but if her lungs were not processing the air intake correctly, the surrounding machines needed to artificially feed her lungs the oxygen at higher saturation levels just to reach the levels necessary for her body to function properly. However, if administered for too long, these higher oxygen percentages could have grave consequences, like blindness and permanent lung damage.

Then just as the gap for the dark oxygen horse passes by, comes the Apnea horse, representing those terrifying moments when Faith forgets to breathe, followed by the Brady horse, which trots by when Apnea has lasted long enough to cause her heart rate to drop to dangerously low levels. Meanwhile every single one of these horses were not only circling around and around but also rising and falling, soaring up and plunging down. The effect...dizzying.

This fun, lighthearted carousel ride for my girls had morphed for me into a mentally freakish, out-of-control excursion I couldn't get off. Peeling my eyes away from its rhythm, I motioned to Erin that I was going to take a walk until they were done. As I strode away, my legs lead my body in straight lines through the mall, but my mind spun. Up and down. Round and round. The faster I walked, the quicker the mental revolutions. Up, down, up, down, round and round.

Will we ever get off this ride? Will Faith make it off the carousel alive? She was a little over a week old, and we still had months to go before she'd be released from the hospital. How would she make it through? How would we make it through?

The next set of questions were the familiar horses of pain and confusion I could not seem to get away from. God, I'm not asking You why this is happening to our family. I realize sometimes bad things happen in life. More so, I'm asking what is Your plan and purpose in this? I realize I've asked You this before, but I'm not sure You've answered it. And If You have, then I haven't understood. I need You to answer me again. What are You doing through all of this, and if Your plan is perfect, why is all this happening now? Why did Faith come when she did?

The yearning in my soul to know the answers was a deep ache. Thankfully that ache was interrupted by a more mundane question.

"Where'd you go?" Erin was breathless as she approached me with Rebekah in tow. "You just took off!"

"I needed to stretch my legs," I answered, as I kissed my wife, then turned my focus on Rebekah. "How did you like the horsies?"

My sweet daughter belly-laughed as I tickled her. I loved that sound.

The rest of our Sunday was filled with the round and round rhythm. After dinner and a bath for Rebekah, we gathered in her room for story time and prayers. As Erin was reading to Rebekah, her voice faded out, and the carousel in my mind circled back to my previous questions. Why now? What is the purpose? Round and Round.

A new thought circled around, blanketing my thoughts. Not so much as a new idea, but more like a remembering of something I already knew. It was a Bible verse, one of my favorite prayers to pray over Rebekah, and one I'd heard quoted at many baptisms and baby dedications. It was a verse that blanketed the truth of our hearts over Faith that read, *"And Jesus grew in wisdom and stature, and in favor with God and man."*

If there was any more appropriate verse for what we wanted to happen in Faith's life, my weak Biblical scholar knowledge did not know it. We wanted four things for her: to be wise, to have a great stature (which we really needed right now as she barely weighed two pounds), to have favor with God, and to have favor with man. But none of those things seemed possible unless she could survive the storm she was currently in. So it seemed like a very appropriate verse to declare over her...every single day until it came to pass.

Wanting to pray it now over Rebekah, I reached for a Bible. Where was that verse? I knew it was in Luke, and it was in the chapter where Mary and Joseph lost Jesus for a few days because He had stayed behind in the Temple to ask questions. I flipped to chapter two and slid my index finger down the page until I found it. Verse 52. Luke 2:52.

I stared at those numbers for a moment. 2:52. If I just moved the colon over, it would be 25:2.

Huh. Faith was born at 25 weeks and 2 days. 25:2.

That could not be a coincidence. I knew in my heart God was answering my prayer, right here and now.

"Erin, would you mind it if I went to go visit Faith?"

"Right now?"

"Yeah, I need to tell her something, and you look snuggled in there with Rebekah. How about you finish bedtime, and I will be back soon?"

Erin nestled into Rebekah's covers and pulled her in close. Smiling, Erin said, "Only if you give us both kisses before you go."

I was happy to oblige.

CHAPTER TWENTY-FIVE

Dreams

Guess what? I am just over a week old, I'm weighing in at just over two pounds, and I am mostly remembering to breathe every day. Life is good! And just to think that the doctors told my mommy and daddy that I would have a zero percent chance of living. I think I'm pretty much winning Olympic gold in this thing called life. My daddy thinks so, too, because he's the one who told me that. I don't even know what Olympic gold is.

Daddy visited me tonight, and it was a very, very special time. I always love when he talks to me; the sound of his voice is so comforting. But then there are times when his voice changes and, I don't know, it's different. It's like when he's talking normal, I love the sound, but then when he prays or speaks about God, it's different and not something I know how to explain. Maybe it's because I'm not old enough to know the right words. But I will try.

When I was still inside my mommy's belly, I couldn't hear words clearly like I can now. I just could hear muffled voices and vibrations and they would make me feel all kinds of things, happy, or sad, or strong. But then there were times when the vibrations would almost fill me up from the inside and those vibrations would help me grow. Like, the actual sounds had power and would help my body...almost like my brain and my lungs were obeying the vibrations. Like their voices were joined with another voice.

When Daddy prayed over me tonight, it felt like that. I know it's just him standing there, and it's hard to understand, but when he prays or talks about Jesus, it's like someone else is there with him.

First, he told me all about what Mommy, Rebekah, and he did today, and he got me really excited to get out of here so I can ride the pretty horses up and down. That sounded like so much fun. And while he talked about that stuff, it was just him. It was just his voice only. But then things changed.

Daddy told me he'd been asking God to talk to him about why I came when I did, and he wanted God to help him know I was just right and arrived in God's perfect time. He told me that sometimes he doubts, and that I probably would too, and that it's okay as long as you just talk about those doubts to God. Then he told me he was going to pray words from the Bible over me, and that's when I felt that special vibration. All of a sudden, I felt like there were way more people standing over me than just Daddy.

Daddy prayed Jesus would personally see to it that I would grow up to have wisdom and favor with God and any person who meets me. And then he prayed I would be strong in something called stature, and when he said those words, I felt my body and my lungs and my belly obeying those words. It was like magic. Better than magic, actually. It was the same thing I would feel inside my mommy, and then I realized that all those times, before I was born, must've been times that Mommy and Daddy were praying for me.

All I could think was that I couldn't wait until I was big enough to have my own voice to pray. Maybe I could one day pray for my mommy and daddy, and they would feel these wonderful vibrations, too. I have an idea ... why don't you pray for my Mommy and Daddy for me? Since I can't speak for myself, you could be the ones speaking for me. That is a great idea!

And to be honest, that is not totally my idea. I heard some nurses talking the other day about this man who used his voice to speak up for some people that could not speak for themselves. He even got a whole bunch of other people to speak up for these people too. And all these people started speaking so often and so loudly that they eventually got some really important people to not just speak, but to actually do something. And from what I learned from my nurses, this man became so important that they gave him his very own day. Now that is pretty cool. They also said that he had a dream of some sort. I guess it had to be a good dream if he was able to do all that.

Well, speaking of dreams, I think I am going to snuggle myself into my little box here in the NICU for the night. As I drift off to sleep, with the backdrop of all these beeps and hustle and bustle, I am going to dream of a day when all of our voices are joined together to talk to the most important Man there is and when all of our voices end up making a difference. They might not give us a day all to ourselves, but if we can see some of our buddies get out of NICU and home to their mommies and daddies, then that will probably be even better than having our very own day.

"Speak up for those who cannot speak for themselves, for the rights of all who are destitute."

Proverbs 31:8

CHAPTER TWENTY-SIX
Elevators

Elevator rides can be awkward, especially when a stranger enters with you on floor ten and the entire descent to the lobby is silent. It's not so bad if there are several people because it's as if everyone has made a secret pact to mind their own business. But when it's just me and someone else, and there's more than a floor or two to go, I get nervous. Trapped inside a tiny metal box as it plummets to the earth, why is it so difficult to say hi? Hospital elevators can be even worse. I never know whether to reach out or give the person space. What if the last thing they want is to tell a stranger their issues?

On this particular night, as I was leaving the NICU, I stepped into the empty elevator, happy to ride with ease to the garage level. Until a hand slipped into the closing door, forcing it to slide open. No big deal. I can just act like I'm texting someone. Except, when I shot a glance over to the guy, he looked familiar. Where had I seen him before?

Oh no.

It was the Rolling Stones Dad of the baby whom I had mistaken as Faith that first night she was born. Awkward. Only a couple times since that embarrassing encounter had I caught glimpses of him in passing, but we had never had an opportunity to actually speak or meet. And I was glad about that. He probably thought I was some kind of weird preemie stalker. I kept my eyes on my phone while I sent a very long text message to myself.

We rode together the entire way down to the garage levels, and as luck would have it, when the door opened to my level, he got off with me. Nice. I jetted out first and strode to my truck, only to hear him following me. Why was he following me? Was his car really down here, or was he the weird stalker finally exacting his revenge against me? I picked up the pace and, just seconds before I unlocked my car, the guy called out.

"Hey…" I heard him addressing me. Could I act like I didn't hear him? Should I make a run for it? "Your name is Blake, right?"

There was no way out of this now. Might as well face my fate.

"Can I help you?" I asked matter-of-factly, but also with a hint of my most manly voice sprinkled in. To my surprise, as I turned and looked at this man for the first time directly in his face, I was met with the kindest of eyes. Softening my tone, I asked, "Is there anything I can help you with?"

"Do you remember me?" he asked with a slight grin.

I couldn't help but chuckle. "Yeah, you're the father of the baby I thought was mine. I'm so sorry about that. That was the first time I'd been able to see our daughter, and after all that had happened the night before, I was pretty out of it."

"Don't even think about it," he answered, smiling broadly as he extended his hand. "I'm Jack, and you certainly don't need to explain. You had the same shell-shocked look all of us have on those first days. Shoot, my wife and I have been here for several months and sometimes I still feel shell-shocked."

"Several months?" Compassion exploded from my chest. "What's your child's name, and how is she doing?"

Jack and Ainsley's story differed greatly from ours. Unlike our journey of weeks of bleeding and cramping, midnight emergency room scares, and extended bedrest, their pregnancy had been progressing along perfectly until one day everything changed. Experiencing sudden pains, Ainsley was rushed to the hospital where their baby, Mary Beth, was born at twenty-six weeks and three days. Even though Mary Beth—we mostly call her MB—was a little bigger than Faith when she arrived, this preemie dealt with serious problems from the start. Even now, months later, she still lived in the NICU, struggling to breathe and eat. Jack talked about the strange rhythm of the NICU and the dichotomy parents feel from day to day. The guilt of not spending enough time at the hospital. The guilt of not spending enough time with their other children. The worry of their baby dying. The worry of their baby living with terrible birth defects. These words were like a mirror into my soul.

"It's like you've snuck into my house and read my journals," I joked. "Erin and I have had every one of these conversations, and Faith is not even two weeks old."

"It's a crazy rollercoaster, up and down, isn't it? Some days, we think we're finally making progress, and then in a heartbeat, the rug is jerked from us and Mary Beth is fighting for her life. She had been on a ventilator for weeks, then right before Faith arrived, she got to go off of it. Ainsley and I were ecstatic. Then last night, MB slid down into a pattern of Bradys and we almost lost her. She had to go back on the vent."

"Jack, I am so sorry to hear that." I sighed and leaned my back against my truck. How had this family had the perseverance to ride this NICU rollercoaster for months? Faith had only been there just shy of two weeks and I was exhausted. However, as Jack shared, I expected to see a broken man, a worn-out, bitter wreck. That's not what I witnessed here in the concrete bowels of the hospital. He seemed strong. Undaunted. I wondered how his voice and demeanor was filled with such hope and concern at the same time? All I could offer was, "I want you to know that Erin and I will pray for you and Ainsley and Mary Beth."

"Thank you. That really means the world to us...and actually, that is why I wanted to meet you." He seemed a bit hesitant to say the rest. "You know that our areas in the NICU aren't the most private, right?"

"What, you mean those curtain dividers aren't soundproof?" I asked sarcastically.

"Exactly." He smiled. "I just wanted to thank you for what I heard you speaking over Faith. MB had just been put back on the ventilator, Ainsley had already left to go home that night, and I was just sitting there staring at my baby girl. The wind had been sucked out of our sails."

I nodded. I knew that feeling.

"I wasn't trying to eavesdrop or anything. In fact, I'm not sure I've ever really heard you and your wife talking over in your area before, but it was like your words for Faith were also for MB, for me, too. I heard them as clear as a bell. When you talked to her about her coming at just the perfect time, and that God knew what he was doing, and then you prayed with such faith for her to grow in stature and favor with God and man...I don't know... it was exactly what I needed to hear. It was like a fresh wind blew through, and I could breathe again. I just wanted to meet you tonight and thank you for being such a great man of faith."

I was speechless.

How could this man think this about me? I felt like a private being complimented by a general. If this man had only known how many nights I'd stayed awake wondering if God was even listening, how heavily enshrouded with doubt I felt, how small and ill-equipped I believed I was, would he have walked all this way to say these words to me? Now, my wife, she deserved all this; Erin's faith had been unshakeable ever since the night God spoke to her and named our baby Faith. But me? I struggled. One minute feeling strong, the next minute curled in the fetal position, hiding under my bed in defeat.

"I don't know what to say, Jack," I said, unable to meet his eyes. "Honestly, I don't feel like a great man of faith."

Jack sat down on the bumper of my truck as we allowed the silence of the parking garage to invade our conversation. Tires squeaked in the distance against the sharp turns of the exit ramps. The cold concrete around us smelled damp.

"Blake," Jack resumed, "I can't tell you how many times I've felt the same way. And that's when God reminds me that faith isn't a feeling. I'm not so sure that our faith isn't the strongest when we have so much doubt and choose to pray anyway, right? It's easy to pray when we feel strong. It's a little harder when life is a dumpster fire."

My eyes burned with tears. I was not sure if my voice would hold steady if I spoke, so I simply nodded my head. After several deep breaths, I said, "It helps so much to have people like you... praying with us...people who understand what it's like."

After exchanging numbers, I invited Jack to check out our CaringBridge site, only to find out he and his wife had also been using this platform as a channel of communication.

"Take the time to read the comments people write," he advised. "I mean, really read them and allow the words to sink in. We've had people we've never met leave us the most generous messages. At first, I'd just breeze over them, thinking they were just being nice. But then, the Lord nudged me with the thought that He was using these friends and strangers to send words of encouragement, and I needed to honor them. I cannot tell you how much they've helped me and Ainsley."

Shaking hands goodbye, I thanked him again for hunting me down, joking about how relieved I was that he hadn't intended punch me for lurking over his baby girl. We laughed, and I promised to take his advice about the CaringBridge pages to heart. And I quietly made a promise to the Lord to listen more carefully to His promptings when riding in elevators, especially in the hospital. By just a word, the awkwardness could transform into a blessing.

CHAPTER TWENTY-SEVEN

Failure to Thrive

The oversized, vibrant photos of the children greeted me like a welcoming parade. This hallway leading me to the UAB neonatologist offices seemed more like a proud grandparent's photo wall of fame than an entrance to a hospital wing. All the sunny smiles and faces emanated joy as each poster listed the child's birthday, weight, and gestational age at birth. There was curly-headed Langston, born at twenty-seven weeks, three days, weighing in at two pounds, thirteen ounces, now around five years old and proudly wearing his firefighter's outfit. Next was pre-teen Olivia, with a face full of freckles, laughing with her two older sisters. She was born at thirty-one weeks, one day, and weighed in at three pounds, two ounces. I couldn't believe Jordan was born a preemie, as his photo displayed him now as a burly high school football player. But sure enough, his information said he'd been born at twenty-five weeks, two days, and only weighed two pounds at birth! His virile stature filled me with hope for my girl, who had the exact same gestational age.

Opening the glass doors to the offices, I scanned the room. A few doctors and nurses casually chattered in the corner, and the one laughing the most was a female doctor wearing pink cowgirl boots underneath her scrubs. She seemed like the kind of happy soul I'd want watching over my baby.

"Mr. Hamby!" I couldn't believe Dr. Carlo had been watching for me to arrive. "So good to see you," he said, reaching out his hand. "Thank you for making time to come and visit on such short notice."

"It's me who should thank you for making room in your schedule," I insisted as we shook hands. "And please, Dr. Carlo, please call me Blake."

Ever since my first conversation with Dr. Carlo, I hadn't been able to get UAB out of my mind, kind of like the stray thread on the corner of your shirt that you can't help but tug. But the more you pulled on it, the more you created additional stray threads.

Failure to Thrive

Would Faith be better off here? Could Dr. Carlo help in ways our current doctors couldn't? Did UAB live up to its reputation of cutting edge NICU practices? A thread I could not leave alone was the notion that there had to be a higher level of neonatology innovation than the Saran-wrapped plastic box my daughter slept in. My curiosity finally overshadowed a feeling of guilt about looking elsewhere. So I'd called Dr. Carlo and asked for a tour.

"All these photos of kids who were born premature are so encouraging." I nodded to the hallway.

"We love seeing those smiling faces." Dr. Carlo beamed. "When we first opened the new NICU about seven years ago, the March of Dimes gave us the idea. They thought it would bring hope to the families here if they saw pictures of others who had progressed in life. But what we didn't realize is how much it would bring hope to us all, the doctors and nurses, as we served the families and cared for the babies."

With every word, I loved Dr. Carlo more. What I wanted to do was wrap this man in a massive bear hug and drench his lab coat with my tears. What I did was casually ask, "Whoever the March of Dimes is, they got this one hundred percent right."

"Oh, you need to know who they are," Dr. Carlo smiled. "They are a great organization that works all across the country with families who are dealing with premature babies. They're very active in our NICU, and they stock the family rooms with food, toys, and even counselors if the parents need them. Let me show you around the place."

As I listened to Dr. Carlo host the next forty minutes of the tour, I imagined this was what it must've been like to have Walt Disney as a Disneyland guide. His eyes gleamed as he shared his vision about why he and his team had designed this unit the way they did. Every detail was intentional, from the nurse stations to the parent rooms to the flow of traffic to the individual wings. Each baby had a private room with a small area for parents to sleep and shower. And the only Saran wrap I saw in the entire place was wrapped around a nurse's sandwiche.

Unable to ignore that nagging thread dangling in my mind, I asked Dr. Carlo about the details of our present situation, Faith's progress, and her current care. While he didn't address the Saran wrap, he did spend time asking questions, after which he ended up validating every aspect of Faith's care. He reassured me that her doctors were doing exactly what they would do at UAB. Just then, my phone went off.

"Why don't you take that while I check in with one of my colleagues?" Dr. Carlo said as he walked toward a doctor who was motioning toward him. "I'll be back in a few minutes."

Erin's picture filled my phone screen.

"What's up?" I asked.

"Sock, we need to pray." The urgency in her voice struck fear into my heart.

"What's going on? When I left Faith this morning, she was doing well."

"Everything's changed. I just spent an hour with her, and in that time alone, she had three Bradys and her oxygen is up to 40%." I could hear the tightness in Erin's voice. "The doctor said she wasn't thriving."

"What does that mean, 'thriving?' Is that a medical term?"

"I don't know, Blake, but it's not good. We need to pray."

Sitting down in the nearest chair, I bowed my head to pray with Erin. When I looked up, Dr. Carlo was sitting next to me, eyes also closed, quietly agreeing with us.

"Is there a problem with Faith?" he asked gently once I hung up.

"Faith is having trouble breathing. Bradys. 40% oxygen." I sighed deeply. "Her doctor said she wasn't thriving. I don't even know what that means."

"Failure to thrive could mean many things." Dr. Carlo switched into doctor mode. "And that term has a spectrum. But basically it means Faith isn't progressing as we desire her to. But, Blake, with preemies, that status could change in a matter of a hours. I know each day brings its own set of challenges, but these issues are normal for your baby. Just give it time and have faith." Dr. Carlo's eyes resonated with such a depth of compassion and confidence.

"Thank you," I said as I stood. "For your time today, and for your prayers."

After Dr. Carlo disappeared into his office, my feet felt anchored to the floor. No part of me wanted to step outside this hospital and into the future unknowns with Faith as she fought for her life. Surrounded by the bright and hopeful faces that plastered these walls, kids who had survived their NICU journey and were now thriving, discovering their purposes, I felt so conflicted. These same photos that greeted me upon entering and filled me with hope, now seemed to mock me, teasing me of a future I desperately wanted for Faith. But from where I stood right now, that future seemed like an impossibility. I had to force my feet to shuffle toward my truck.

As I drove to meet Erin for a visit with Faith before going home to Rebekah, a piece of my heart stayed behind at UAB's Disneyland NICU. Now that I had walked their halls, I wanted more than ever to have Dr. Carlo and doctors who wore pink cowgirl boots to care for my baby girl.

CHAPTER TWENTY-EIGHT

Burdens

Tonight both my mommy and daddy visited me, tucked me in and said our bedtime prayers. They told me that once I came home, I could not stay up late like this, so I'd better take advantage of these late-night chats while I can.

Have I told you yet that it's my favorite thing when both of them are here? I feel so snuggly and safe when I can hear both their voices and it reminds me of before. Before it was always nice and dark and warm and I could always hear my mommy's heartbeat. That was the best thing ever. Oh! And I could also hear when my mommy and daddy would laugh. I love to hear them laugh. Another thing that was good about before was that I didn't have to breathe. Maybe that's why out here I am not doing this breathing thing so well.

Out here, it can be so bright. And really loud with all the beeping. And sometimes cold. But that's probably because I pretty much lie around naked all day. Mommy says she cannot wait to doll me up in pretty dresses. That sounds like fun and really makes me want to grow up and go home. But I have to learn to breathe first, and like I said, I'm not very good at that yet. I heard the doctor tell my mommy that I wasn't thriving, and she immediately called Daddy so they could pray. Her voice sounded like she was worried about what the doctor said.

So, the last couple of days have been hard, and that's also why it was so comforting to have both my parents with me at the same time. Their prayers make me feel strong. And I need that right now. Their prayers make something inside me feel I will eventually get good at the breathing. A hope, I think it's called.

It's not that I don't want to breathe; it's just that I keep forgetting. And when that happens, a couple beeps go off, and this stuff called oxygen goes out of my body and then my heart stops beating like it should. Then all kinds of alarms go off. They sound like they are coming from all around me.

Usually, the nurse can just give me a little pat on my back, and that reminds me to breathe. But sometimes, I just can't seem to do it, no matter how hard I try. So then even more alarms go off, if you can believe that, and the nurses have to squeeze this bag-balloon thing over my mouth to force me to breathe and then I finally can catch my breath. But if that still doesn't work, then they put this thing called caffeine in my body. That usually does the trick. Daddy made me feel a little better when he told me he needs to have caffeine every day, too. I wonder if that means he has trouble breathing sometimes, too?

Between you and me, I don't like it. The whole thing. It's kind of scary for me. I wish I could just tell my lungs to do what they are supposed to do. And that they would obey.

Anyway, could you please keep praying for me? Pray that my lungs will obey. It means so much that you come here to read my entries...but even more that you pray. Mommy and Daddy told me how much y'all are praying for me, and I know that is why I have hope inside me. Even when it gets scary.

And could I also ask another favor? Please remember to keep praying for all of my buddies here. Especially a girl named Mary Beth. I heard Mommy and Daddy talking with Mary Beth's parents, and she is on a thing called a ventilator. It's a good thing but also a bad thing, which I don't really understand. The best I could figure out is that it helps her breathe and gives her the oxygen she needs, but it also can hurt her lungs. How can something be good and bad at the same time? Please pray she gets the good stuff from the ventilator, but not the bad stuff. She's a lot older than me and I heard Mommy whisper to Daddy that she should've been out of here a long time ago. Let's pray that she gets strong and that she can go home soon.

Well, that is enough of all that for tonight, I guess. I am going to drift off to sleep now and get ready for what I hope is a nice, restful weekend. As I drift off to sleep, I will pray that sometime this weekend you will take time to rest a bit and spend time with someone you love. I have learned that just for my mom and dad to come and sit in a chair beside my box is really special and it makes me feel needed. It even makes me want to work harder on this breathing thing so I can go home with them and spend even more time together doing more than just stare at each other. I hope when I go home that me and my family don't forget how special it is to just be together. I hear it is busy out there in the world and that sometimes adults forget to just stop and spend time together.

So for you to spend a little time with me on our site is just super duper and makes me feel all warm inside, like when my mommy and daddy come to visit me!

"Carry each other's burdens, and in this way you will fulfill the law of Christ."

Galatians 6:2

CHAPTER TWENTY-NINE

Ventilator

My first thought when I woke was wondering why there was a heavy weight on my chest. I couldn't seem to get my breath. Had I even slept at all last night? Really slept? Even my dreams were visions of fitful sleep, checking the clock every twenty minutes. Draping my arm around my deeply slumbering wife, I was thankful for a lazy Saturday morning. Maybe I could score an hour or two more of sleep before Rebekah pounced into our bed. But even snuggled next to my beautiful, peaceful wife, I couldn't loosen the imaginary bands that seemed to constrict my chest.

These last few days had felt like a month, every day wrought with ups and downs, just without the ups, only downs. Was this pressure in my lungs how Faith felt in her box when she spiraled into Bradys, unable to breathe deeply? Why was she not improving the way we craved?

Realizing sleep would not come, I decided a run would do me good. Slipping out of bed and leaving a note for Erin, I dressed and hit the pavement. The icy January air burned my throat and lungs as my body attempted to adapt to the drastic change in temperature. Just moments before, I'd been toasty under the sheets with my wife; why did I think a winter run was a good idea? Especially on an empty stomach and no coffee.

But my feet pounded out a rhythm, one I'd followed countless times, and before I knew it, I was lost in the familiar tempo of my pace. Right, left, right, left. I could always count on running. Many questions had haunted me over the last several weeks, unknowns that might never become knowns. After about a mile, my lungs released their grip and opened with the cold morning air. I wished I could feel this clarity of mind and breathe all day, every day.

Without planning it, I found my legs leading me along the miles of back roads to the hospital, toward Faith. Once again, I was grateful we lived fairly close to our baby's NICU. How do parents of preemies handle living far away, endure the many long, late night commutes home after a full day's work and an intense visit with their baby? Or to the NICU when their baby has a midnight emergency, during which every second is life or death?

Once I arrived at the hospital, I went to the coffee shop to cool down, warm up, dry off, and most importantly, get coffee and a sandwich.

"How's our little Faith doing?" a friendly voice behind me asked.

"Jack," I said. "Have a seat."

"Did you run here?" He looked surprised.

"We're only a few miles away, and I needed to clear my head."

"So let me ask again," he asked knowingly. "How is Faith doing?"

My eyes drifted to my coffee, and Jack was patient as I gathered my thoughts.

"The last few days have been rough, Jack. She can't seem to find her rhythm with breathing. Her oxygen levels are up, and she's been having Bradys every day."

"Those are rough days; Ainsley and I know them well. How's Erin?"

The kindness and thoughtfulness of Jack lifted my spirits. "Erin is a rock. Sure, she feels the emotion like any mom would, but I am constantly amazed at how firm her faith is. Her trust in

God and belief He will bring Faith through this is unshakable."

"Wow," Jack said. "That's a blessing. Maybe we should encourage her and my wife to join forces. They could take over the world."

I laughed at the truth of his suggestion. "How is Mary Beth?"

"Still on the ventilator. It just isn't working for her like we need it to."

My heart sank for them, and my chest felt a tinge of the tightness from earlier that morning.

After a brief silence, Jack asked, "Are you coming or going?"

"I actually haven't seen Faith yet. After running here, I needed some coffee."

Smiling, Jack stood and said, "I know you know this, but we are praying and will continue to pray."

"Us too," I said and shook his hand goodbye.

Making my way up to the NICU, I stood outside the door for several moments, hesitant to face what condition Faith might be in. *Jesus, give me the strength I need.*

When the nurse greeted me, she was positive, as usual, but the beeps and the monitors clearly communicated that Faith wasn't getting the oxygen she needed. In fact, her oxygen intake read 100%. Again, I felt hints of the chest constriction I'd woken up with.

"I really do appreciate how positive your entire team is," I said

Ventilator

sincerely. "But this level of oxygen isn't where we want it to be, is it?"

"No, Mr. Hamby," the nurse answered. "But this happens with a lot of preemies. In most all cases, they need to spend time on a ventilator. They just have such—"

"I'm sorry...ventilator? What do you mean? Is Faith on one now?"

My alarm must have been strong because her focus switched to the defensive.

"No, no, no, no, Mr. Hamby. I promise that would never happen without letting you know." She smiled broadly to calm me down. "Besides, even if she were, you would notice it right away."

"What do you mean?"

"Well, a ventilator is there to help the baby breathe, so it's a bit of a contraption, and there would be more tubes. One in her mouth...that goes down her throat."

My expression must've gone ghostly because she backed off, quickly adding before slipping away, "Dr. Armando will be here to answer any questions you might have."

I wished I was still outside running. Maybe all the way to Mexico.

When Dr. Armando arrived, I was staring blankly at Faith.

After the normal cordial doctor/patient updates, he began talking about the next steps, and the virtues of the ventilator. His words were like a bitter medicine; no matter how much cherry flavor you use to mask the true flavor, the aftertaste is still brutal.

"How necessary is this?" I asked, feeling defeated. "And what are the risks?"

"Faith's body is working so hard just to breathe, and she still is not getting the oxygen she needs. The ventilator will give her body a break and will help every part of her—her brain, her organs—get the oxygenated nutrients they need. It will help her body grow and mature."

"Okay," was all I could say as I prepared myself to ask my next question, the one I did not want the answers to. "And the risks?"

"When oxygen is forced directly into her lungs, there can be issues. Her lungs are very delicate, and while the rest of her body would benefit, her lungs could be damaged, potentially scarred for life. And if she is on the ventilator for a prolonged amount of time, there could be eye damage as well."

"What do you mean?"

"Possible blindness."

"How long will she be on the ventilator?"

Dr. Armando looked me straight in the eyes. "There is no way of knowing. It could be a couple of days. Could be a few weeks."

The medicine this doctor administered through his words proved more than my stomach could handle.

"Thank you for your honesty." I think my voice was noticeably higher than usual. "Please excuse me for a moment. I need to run to the bathroom."

"Of course," he answered. "I will be on the floor for the next few hours, so please don't hesitate to come and find me if you have questions." As he walked away, I thought about how I was going to be on the floor for the next few hours also, just not in the same manner he was referring to.

I quickly hid myself in a nearby bathroom, one that was a single room and would offer me privacy, so I could throw up the breakfast I'd just eaten. Then I sat on the cold tile with my head in my hands and wept.

CHAPTER THIRTY

Disney World

click, click, click, click This is the new sound I hear all day, all night. *click, click, click, click* It's the sound of the ventilator that is helping me breathe. *click, click, click, click* The rhythm is all around me, all the time, in my waking hours and in my dreams.

click, click, click, click My daddy told me that sound reminds him of this place called Space Mountain that is found in a magical place called Disney World. He said this Space Mountain makes that sound right before it shoots you off on a wild adventure. Daddy said Space Mountain is a roller coaster, and it takes you on an exciting and fast ride full of twists and turns. He told me you go up really high and then unexpectedly you shoot way down low. Then the next thing you know, the ride jerks you to the left and right and back again. And, the real kicker is that it does all this without you knowing what is coming next because you are totally in the dark!

I told Daddy that did not sound like any place I wanted to go, but then he told me about all the princesses at Disney World and that sounded much more fun. In Disney World, he said that little kids are magically turned into heroic princes and princesses who fight against all the dark and scary things. He also told me about all these special characters that are there to help you, like fairies and clowns and talking mice. He said they were not scary at all, but they were all there to help make sure you had a wonderful and safe visit. And the best part is that each day ends with a celebration that is fit for the best day of your life. I'll have to say that place sounded much better than the Space Mountain place. My last few days here have been as unpredictable as the speedy highs and sudden lows of that ride. And I don't like it at all. *click, click, click, click*

Well, so much for all that. Let's get down to the business of giving you an update on life here in the box. This morning there was a short period when I didn't hear the clicks because the doctor tried to take me off the ventilator. The only way to see if my lungs are strong enough and my body is ready to breathe on its own is to test it out. Daddy said it was like the Safari Ride at Animal Kingdom, which is apparently at this Disney place too. As long as I stayed in the vehicle, I was safe, but the moment I stepped off, there were lions and tigers ready to chase me all over the place.

So... *click, click, click, click* I've been put back on the vent until further notice.

All in all, I really would ask you to pray for my ability to breathe. The sooner I can learn that, the sooner I can come home and meet all my new buddies, like you! Maybe we could all go to that Disney place together? Also, the longer I stay on this ventilator, the worse it is for my lungs. The doctor says I already have something called chronic lung disease and the more I have to use this ventilator, the worse off my lungs could be. And my eyes.

I have to admit, all this talk of scary things makes me feel lost and alone and makes me want to run away from this place and go to the magical part of the Disney World my daddy talked about. But the more I think about it, I guess in some ways I am closer to this magical place than I realized. The way my mommy and daddy love me makes me feel like a princess. And I know the other little kids in here with me sure seem like they are heroes that are fighting against some dark forces. And our nurses and doctors and the receptionists and people that help keep this place clean sure seem like they are all there to make our stay as safe and enjoyable as possible. And while there might be twists and turns and it sure feels like we are lost sometimes and flying in the dark, I have to admit, when I get to the end of each day, I feel like I have my own little reasons to celebrate. I get to end each day by reading all the wonderful things you all wrote. Even on the days when I am just too tired to read them, I am able to snuggle all my two pounds into my warm little box and know that I did the best I could and that I fought a good fight and God gave me one more day to experience this great big and beautiful and magical thing called life. When I choose to look at things that way, I guess that is worthy of a little celebration.

While I am snuggled in tonight having my own little celebration for making it through another day, I will also pray for you. I'll pray that whatever dark twists and turns or ups and downs you might have had to walk through that you will find a little of magic that is so often hiding just beyond the scary parts of our days.

click, click, click, click

Where can I go from your Spirit? Where can I flee from your presence? If I go up to the heavens, you are there; if I make my bed in the depths, you are there. If I rise on the wings of the dawn, if I settle on the far side of the sea, even there your hand will guide me, your right hand will hold me fast. If I say, "Surely the darkness will hide me and the light become night around me," even the darkness will not be dark to you; the night will shine like the day, for darkness will not be dark to you; the night will shine like the day, for darkness is as light to you. For you created my inmost being; you knit me together in my mother's womb. I praise you because I am fearfully and wonderfully made; your works are wonderful, I know that full well.

Psalm 139: 7–14

CHAPTER THIRTY-ONE

Days Revisited

There are days I would choose to relive in a heartbeat: The day I met Erin at the Trak Shak and thought she'd be the last woman on the planet that I'd fall in love with. The day I realized how wrong I'd been, how passionately I loved her, and how I could never fully live my life if I didn't have her by my side. The day Rebekah was born. (The day Rebekah was conceived was a good one too). The day we found out Erin was pregnant with Faith. So many holidays that were full of laughter and adventure. Or Sundays at church, where I tangibly felt the presence of God. Or nights I will never remember, with friends I will never forget. I have been blessed with countless days that I would revisit if ever given the chance.

But there is one particular day I would never repeat.

I'd finished early at work, which was a surprise considering how much time I had been spending outside the office and inside the NICU. But there I sat, behind my desk, rifling through pages to unearth undone work. Surely there was more to do, another spreadsheet to work on, or a past meeting to notate. Anything to keep my mind occupied on a task at hand and away from my baby in the hospital.

The past several days for Faith had been difficult ones. Since the last failed attempt to remove her from the ventilator, she showed no signs of even being close to breathing independently. The NICU staff continued to keep the oxygen levels around 50% to 70% which meant Faith was struggling mightily to properly oxygenate herself without artificial help. Because our baby was still not thriving, Dr. Armando had another sit-down with Erin and me about the possible repercussions of long-term ventilator use. Blindness. Lung damage. While there was no way to un-hear those frightening words, or try to drown them out with piles of office work, that didn't stop me from trying.

I shuffled and re-shuffled the papers on my desk until I surrendered to the reality that my office work was done. Perhaps by reflex, I dialed the hospital to check on Faith and was discouraged to be informed that her white blood cell count was high, a strong indication of an infection somewhere in her tiny body.

On top of the news that her lungs were still showing no sign of improvement, I knew an infection could compound many issues for our tiny baby. Dread seeped into my heart as I steered my truck toward the NICU.

When I walked into the NICU, very few nurses bustled around, and even fewer parents. Sounds from the many machines that flanked each incubator filled the vacancy. Beeps and clicks and mechanical noises. What was it like for these preemies to leave a dark atmosphere filled only with the organic tones of their mommy's heartbeats and warm vibrations of muffled voices and be thrust into bright fluorescent lights and the electric bleating of monitors?

With Faith's white blood cell count elevated, I was very thankful she had finally been provided a "box" instead of the Saran wrap. However, she looked dwarfed under her box surrounded by the fortress of roll-away monitor walls and the ventilator that made an unwelcome home for itself. I would do anything to switch places with my precious baby girl. Touching her incubator, I prayed.

As soon as words came out of my mouth, her oxygen saturation alarm went off. That was nothing new, so I simply continued talking to God. I thanked Him for Faith, for the support He had generously given us through our friends and family, and even for the growth in me as He walked me through this process. Although I had grown accustomed to the different alarms beeping, I kept her numbers under my supervision, and while I prayed, I watched her vitals slipping downward. Not too much at first, just in the low nineties, then into the upper eighties. Still nothing to freak out about; we had been here before.

When Faith's numbers dropped into the upper seventies, I found it difficult to focus on praying. My words seemed to tumble away with her numbers. At seventy-one, all my words were gone as my eyes darted around, trying to read every single number at once. Down, down, down. When the numbers plummeted into the sixties, I knew she was in trouble. *Don't panic, Blake, just find a nurse. Now!*

Stepping out of our area, I swiveled to catch sight of even one nurse, but the entire room appeared empty. I was trapped. Alone. And I was panicking. I darted back to check the monitors to see if there had been an upward tick, but now Faith's heart rate was half what it should be. *What is happening?*

Running out of our area, I frantically searched for anyone who could help. Still, no one was in sight. For every drop in Faith's heart rate, mine skyrocketed until I could hear my own heart throbbing in my ears. Pivoting sharply, my business shoes slipped on the tile floor, and I almost slammed onto the floor. But I narrowly caught myself on the corner of the receptionist's desk.

"Please, you have to help me," I pleaded. "My daughter needs help."

My panicked face alerted her enough to immediately call the team. But I was too amped up to allow Faith's life to rest solely in her hands. Scrambling to the other side of the NICU, I found several nurses, but by that point, I was so frantic I couldn't speak. All I could hear were the monitors in Faith's area screaming for attention.

"Help!! I need help." I managed to gasp. "My daughter, she's bad. Can you please come?"

Dropping what they were doing, they sprinted toward Faith's space, and as we approached, two more doctors burst out of nowhere as we all ran to Faith's rescue. When we arrived, her monitor with the oxygen saturation read thirty-four, and her heart rate was no better. Everything in me wanted to grab her and breathe life into her lungs, but when I looked down at her face, what I saw terrified me far more than her numbers. Her skin was blue.

Our nurse zipped the curtain to close off our area, and as five medical professionals converged over Faith's tiny body, I slowly backed up to the very edge of the curtain. Opening her box, one doctor grabbed what they refer to as a bag, placed it over Faith's tiny mouth, and aggressively attempted to force air into her mouth and nostrils. They all talked over each other and every person feverishly worked to do what they could to save Faith from this spiral toward death.

Every second was an hour. The burst of adrenaline that had coursed through my veins thickened to despair. This is it. My daughter is dying, right before my eyes. How can this be happening? How can she die right now?

I wanted to pray, I needed to pray, to get the words out that would save Faith. Words that would show enough faith to transform the situation. Opening my mouth, the only word that I managed to breathe out was...Jesus.

Jesus, help.

Jesus. Jesus. Help.

As I whispered those words, I deflated into the corner of this cold and miserable NICU hell that apparently was the only earthly place Faith would ever know. I sank onto the tile and held my legs against my chest and slammed my eyes shut. My mind was bombarded with visions of Faith running through our backyard. Holding her first lost tooth. Riding her bike and playing dolls with Rebekah. Bringing home her first boyfriend. Making us laugh around the dinner table on a normal Tuesday night. I envisioned every normal and extraordinary thing she would never do.

Jesus help.

Engulfed in this tragedy, I curled my head between my knees

and wept. I wept like I imagined Jesus weeping in the garden. I wept like I knew so many other parents had wept when facing the same fate.

Jesus help.

The next thing I knew, a nurse was gently touching the top of my head.

"Mr. Hamby," she whispered.

My head felt one hundred pounds, and I strained to look up at her, dreading to hear her speak the unimaginable words about Faith.

"Mr. Hamby," she said. "Faith...well...that little girl gave us some kind of scare."

"I'm sorry," I closed my eyes to hear her better, "Is she"—I could barely ask—"Is she okay?"

"Yes, she is. She is for now. We think we have her stable." Her smile looked weary. "And I want you to know that I just had a little chat with her, letting her know she need not do this type of thing any longer. Or ever again."

"So..." I dared not to hope. "That is good, right? I mean, she is good?"

"For now, she is good."

As she helped me stand, my rubbery legs wouldn't steady me, and I almost passed out. She led me over to a chair so I could sit, and then she rolled me next to Faith.

"I'll give you two a moment."

Puddles still clung to my eyes as I peered at my baby. Her skin was no longer blue, and her vitals had stabilized. She was alive. At only twenty-nine weeks gestation, this tiny human, this precious gift from God, had lived and fought so hard for one whole month. But her life had nearly been snuffed out without her ever being able to open her eyes and gaze upon this world. This little girl, 100% alive and 100% a real person, I loved her so deeply. How in the world could she ever be taken from us? How would Erin and I ever move forward from a tragedy like that?

"Faith," I whispered. "Today is not a day we want to relive. I mean it. Not when there are so many days ahead of you that will be filled with life and wonder and fun. Those are days to live for, to fight for. You live for those days to look back on and wish you could relive. Do you hear me? Can you promise me we will not relive this day?"

The only answers I received were the beeps and clicks from her machines.

CHAPTER THIRTY-TWO

Losing My Mind

How was I ever going to leave my daughter again? If I had not been there as her numbers crashed, had I not finished my work early, had I not made an unexpected visit to the NICU, had I not been standing next to her at the moment Faith's vitals had plummeted toward certain death, and then had I not run to find the faraway nurses, would my daughter have died? Would anyone have come to rescue her if I had not been there? With these uncertainties, how could Erin or I ever leave Faith's side? We couldn't. No way. We must stand watch. Every day, every night. No matter what the sacrifice, we must protect our baby girl at all costs. 24-7.

As these commands circled inside my head, I knew they would be impossible to obey. Erin needed to take care of Rebekah. I had a job to keep. I certainly couldn't quit or take a leave of absence. Maybe we could create a schedule and get family and friends to help out. The hospital staff had been great but they could not be expected to stand guard over her 24/7. If we didn't take drastic measures, and then Faith ended up dying, how would we live with ourselves knowing we hadn't taken measures to ensure her survival?

My gut churned with anger. Would this have happened if we were at UAB and under Dr. Carlo's care? There were so many nurses that day when I'd toured the facility...why were there not as many here? Where were they today when Faith's monitors were screaming for help? My face flushed with heat, and I had to get out. I didn't trust I would not bite off a nurse's head if she came in to check on Faith, and I needed to keep in good standings with the very people who had just saved her life.

Stepping outside into the winter evening, I saw the faintest light from the sunset, tiny rays on the edges of a horizon packed with overweight rain clouds. I wasn't ready to drive home yet; the anger still coursed through my body, and the cold air felt amazing on my cheeks. A slight, icy mist chilled through my hair.

A buzz sounded from my phone with a call from Erin.

"Hey," I answered.

"Are you driving home from work?" Erin asked.

"No, I got done early, so I stopped by to see Faith." Should I dump on her the entire horror story of what happened in the NICU right now, or wait until I get home? Not sure I was ready to talk about the trauma I'd just experienced, I said. "It's a good thing I was here." I breathed in the frigid air to keep the boil of my anger from erupting as I thought about how Faith had basically died right before my eyes.

"Why is it a good thing? Is everything okay?"

"Faith is okay, and I'm standing outside my truck, so I'll be home in just a couple of minutes to talk about it." Then I remembered: My dad was supposed to drive down to paint our bathroom. He had offered to help us out with this project, and both Erin and I had been grateful for the gesture. "Is Dad there?"

"Oh, he never came," Erin said nonchalantly. "He texted me earlier and said he couldn't get away today and would come later."

"Wait." Surely my dad didn't just bail on us like this? I could almost hear the rage bubbling inside me. "You're joking, right?"

"No, Sock, but it's totally okay. He just couldn't make it, and that bathroom has been needing a paint job for so long...a few more days won't matter."

"Got it," I clipped back. "I'll see you in just a bit."

I hung up. Erin's logic about 'a few more days' had no effect on me. I was hot. He had promised. People needed to follow through on their promises. They needed to be there when you needed them. In my anger, I dialed my dad's number.

"Hey there." I didn't give him a chance to speak. "I thought you were coming to paint the bathroom?"

"Oh, yeah, I'm sorry about that." He didn't sound sorry. "I wasn't able to make it today."

"Did something come up? Are you all right?" I kept my voice measured to hide my irritation.

"No, no, no. I'm totally fine, thank you for asking," he said kindly. "Nothing major came up. I have just been really busy and needed to take care of a few things here before I took the day off."

Are you kidding me? You've been busy?! Those words boiled over a primal rage I had no clue was within me, but I somehow managed to keep them inside, saying instead, "Oh. Hmm. Well, I sure hope you found some rest since you've been so busy." My words dripped with sarcasm. "I totally understand because in case you haven't noticed, I've had a little bit on my plate as well."

"Whoa, wait a minute, son." He answered with grace. "I'm sorry if that offended you. I know you've been going through... well...I cannot imagine what you and Erin have been going through."

His humility was not helping. I wanted a fight, and his gentle answers were not turning away my wrath. Why couldn't he throw back the verbal punches I continued to deliver? I grumbled a few more swings at him, but he wouldn't take the bait. He went so far as to offer some advice that I'm sure I needed, but there was not a chance I was going to bow down now. The boil-over had begun, and if he would not spar, then I didn't want to talk to him anymore.

As soon as I hit end, I paced back and forth in that parking lot like a newly caged panther. Images of Faith's monitors with falling numbers bombarded my mind. No nurses to be found. Then doctors bagging my poor baby's mouth to bring her back to life. And now my own father, when I needed him, could not take the time to help me out. Anger ripped through my throat with a roar as I threw my phone into a clump of shrubs next to my truck, and I took off running.

The icy mist graduated to a drizzling rain as I sprinted out of the parking lot and hit the sidewalks. With no destination in mind, I chased after a new reality. Maybe if I could run far enough and fast enough, I could leave my troubles behind, and my world would come back into order. Perhaps I could marathon to a place where my child would not die.

As I passed a local sports bar and grill, I felt a twinge of jealousy toward the men sitting around the bar talking about who was going to win the AFC championship game that weekend. My eyes stung with tears at the desire to have such a frivolous conversation over a cold beer. I turned the corner onto a road filled with rush hour traffic and noticed several passengers giving me double-takes as I ran by. Maybe it was unusual for a man to be running in the freezing rain during rush hour? Or maybe it was most unusual for a man to be running in the freezing rain wearing a full business suit, dress shoes, and a tie flapping over his shoulder?

But none of them stopped. None of them had been so kind as to roll down a window and ask if I was okay. They just kept driving along toward what I imagined to be their perfect little comfortable lives. In my self-pity, I offered no thought to the reality that many of them were probably coming from or going to or sitting in their very own undeserved hell-on-earth.

Left, right, left, right. I hit a rhythm. Breathe in, breathe out. The efforts of my body slowly metabolized the fuel of my internal inferno. The clouds of irrationality melted away in the comfort of my running pace until the realization of my feet slapping hard on the pavement took front and center. Ouch. Johnston & Murphy calfskin shoes were not made for long distance running. Or for short distance running, for that matter. I slowed to a walk, and my surroundings hugged me with their warm familiarity. I walked the last stretch home, shivering in the rain, and I was finally honest with myself.

I wasn't angry at my dad. Neither was I angry at the NICU

staff. I was furious at my circumstances. Incensed at the death that hung around my precious baby. She had almost lost her life today; I'd watched it play-by-play, unable to save her. Her beautiful face had turned blue. Her fragile body ravaged by the very attempts to save it. I was terrified and deeply hurting. Emotionally bleeding out.

Erin hadn't turned on our porch light yet, and I stood outside our front door unsure of how I would explain what had just happened, how I'd run home in my suit, and why we probably would need to buy me a new iPhone. Sensing a presence at the door, she swung it open, and found me drenched from sweat, rain, and tears. Her eyes moved from relief to see me, to confusion as she scanned me up and down, and finally to love and concern as she read my red-rimmed eyes and realized I might not be okay.

But she didn't say a word. She simply hugged me close, walked me to our master bath shower, pulled a fluffy, fresh towel off the shelf, and told me that when I was ready, she'd be waiting for me with a hot dinner at our kitchen table.

CHAPTER THIRTY-THREE
Beatitudes

Except for the swishing of the wiper blades as they swept aside the freezing rain, the car was silent. Erin and I were engulfed in our own thoughts, both attempting to process the events of the last few hours. After a hot shower, comfortable clothes and a meal, I had relayed the NICU events from earlier that day and my subsequent loss of faculties as I dramatically sprinted home in my dress clothes. The emotion was fresh in the retelling, and we both quietly cried.

We had a profound gratitude for Faith's life being preserved.

At the same time, the thought of the unknown days and weeks ahead brought on a deep weariness. If only those wiper blades could sweep across our lives and push aside the worry, the stress, and most of all the death that seemed to lurk around our baby's incubator.

"What do you think God is doing?" I broke the silence. "Why do you think He is allowing this?" And before she could answer, I shot one more question that had been burning in my mind, "And why are you not losing it? Like, ever? You're always so at peace, and I cannot understand that. Do you sneak out in the middle of the night and scream and cry and drink Scotch in our outdoor shed? Or are you seriously holding it all together as you always seem to be?"

Erin turned the car into the hospital parking lot and searched to find my truck. And hopefully, in the shrubbery next to it, my iPhone. Sliding into a space nearby, she turned off the ignition, clicked off her seatbelt, and swiveled to face me.

"Sock, I don't know what God is doing. I wish I did, but I just don't." She exhaled. "But I do know why I'm not losing my mind." She reached out and took my hands in hers. "Blake, God spoke to me. I know that as I sat in the bathroom in Mobile, before all this got really out of control, He told me this baby would be called Faith."

The rain ticked as it hit the windshield in cold, icy pellets.

"I don't understand why things are happening the way they are," she continued. "I don't know why Faith was born so early, why she is not thriving, why she almost died today, or even where all this is going to end up. But I know God spoke to my heart. And when all the craziness of this roller coaster sends my mind reeling, which it does often, I think back to that bathroom. I remember what God said to me, and I have to believe whatever He gives is good. Right now, no matter what, that is enough. This baby will be called Faith...even if she is only called Faith for a month or a thousand months, God spoke it, and so I believe it. If that means I'm losing my mind, or that I have a silly faith, or that I am not being realistic, then I am ok with that."

Letting go of my hands, Erin reached into the back seat and grabbed her purse. The windshield had fogged as we talked inside the cocoon of her car, the warmth of her words filling my soul. I mulled over what she'd spoken and breathed in the faith they exuded.

"And just when my faith seems too thin, God does something like this." She handed me an envelope with a return address from a church I didn't recognize. The letter rustled as I opened it, and dozens of signatures filled the bottom of the page.

"Eastwood Baptist Church in Monroeville? What is this?" I asked quietly.

"Read it."

"Dear Faith and Family," I read aloud. "We are writing to you with prayers and wishes for you to grow strong and healthy. Tonight at our prayer meeting, Faith, your name was mentioned, and we want you to know that we all prayed for you and your family. We will continue to do so regularly, and we believe God is going to answer all our prayers. You are not alone, and we wanted you to know that."

Tears ran down my face as I realized that of the twenty-eight signatures at the bottom of the letter, I didn't know a single one of them.

"Blake, I have no idea who these people are or how they found out about us. Do we even know anyone who goes to that church?"

My throat was too tight to speak, so I shook my head 'no.' I honestly did not even know there were twenty-eight people in Monroeville.

"This is God," Erin said. "This is all God. He keeps doing stuff like this and that lets me know He has not forgotten us or His promise to us. It's what helps me believe my baby is going to walk out of that hospital. She is going to live and not die. She's going to sit in this car with us, fill our house with a mess and laughter and joy. I don't just believe it, Sock, I know it. I see it. And I am going to keep looking at that until God gives me something else to look at."

After several moments, I finally found my words.

"Thank you, Erin. You're right. About all that you just said, and I want you to know that I don't think you have a silly faith. It's a fierce, childlike faith that takes God at his word, which is exactly the kind of faith Jesus said we need to have. Thank you for reminding me of that."

"What do you think of calling all our friends together for a time of prayer and fasting? These people right here"—I held out the letter from the folks of Eastwood Baptist Church—"this kind of corporate prayer changes things. What if we held a prayer meeting here at the hospital and prayed not just for Faith, but for all these preemies and their families? I'm pretty sure there is a small chapel downstairs that is open 24-7."

Erin's eyes shone with fire. "I love that idea."

I leaned over to kiss my wife and then express my immense gratitude that she was the one walking by my side through this entire season of life.

"You go visit Faith, and I'll be right behind you so we can tuck her in for the night and pray together over her. First, I need to find my iPhone." We both laughed. "And then I want to check out the chapel area, maybe even ask if we need permission to hold a prayer meeting."

Opening the wooden door to the chapel, I stepped into another world. Outside was cold, white and sterile tile, but inside this mini-church, was amber warmth and candles and the smell of polished wooden pews. It was timeless. The bright streetlamps from outside shone through the stained glass, casting colorful rays in streaks across the room.

How many people have lifted prayers from this exact spot over the years? How many languages and nationalities have knelt at this altar and cried out to Jesus, the one true God, for healing or provision or restoration? I felt tangibly surrounded by the enormity of my God and the company of saints as their prayers seemed to hang in the air. I was not alone; God's presence was right here with me.

Prayers spilled from my lips in whispered tones as I thanked Him for His faithfulness and His goodness. It was like talking to a best friend who was so familiar with me that He already knew what I was going to say but listened intently anyway because He simply loved being with me. I sat in a middle pew, closed my eyes, and basked in the comfort of His presence.

After several minutes, I opened my eyes and noticed a large oil painting on the wall. Countless numbers of people gathered on a beautiful green hill, and in the center was Jesus. As He preached, the multitude appeared to be leaning into His words so hard that if they were someone else's words, I don't think they could have stood. But clearly, these were not normal words; in fact, they were much more than mere words. They were life. The embodiment of what the Apostle John wrote:

> *"The Word became flesh and made His dwelling among us"* (John 1:14).

What would it have been like to be on the hill that day? What was the weather like? What did the grass feel like, smell like? Did these people understand the gravity of what was happening right before them?

My eyes drifted to the inscription of this painting, entitled "The Beatitudes," and the following scriptures from the Gospel of Matthew:

> *"Blessed are the poor in spirit, for theirs is the kingdom of heaven.*
> *Blessed are those who mourn, for they will be comforted. Blessed are the meek, for they will inherit the earth. Blessed are those who hunger and thirst for righteousness, for they will be filled"* (Matthew 5:3–6).

Unlike the people in this painting, leaning into the words of Jesus, the words of blessings I'd just read felt to be leaning into me. Words of life, they penetrated my heart in ways I could not describe. Even with unknowns ahead, relief and gratitude washed over me. No definitive answers, yet love and peace remained. Perhaps I also did not truly understand the gravity of what was happening right before me?

CHAPTER THIRTY-FOUR

Dark Places

Guess what? I get to invite you to a very special party! I am so excited, I hardly know what to wear. Okay, that's a little NICU humor because all of us preemies, who are this tiny, only get to wear hats and an itsy-bitsy diaper. But I promise I will break out a super girlie special beanie for tomorrow because my mommy and daddy are not having just one party, they are having two, in one day! And it won't be the same without you being a part of it.

I heard my daddy talking to a nurse one night about some parties he used to go to back in college and how during these parties he would get lost in a bottle. I'm not sure how you do that, but maybe that is because I am a little girl and don't understand adult things yet. But the good news is he said, "The sun started to shine on him while he was lost" and that must have helped him find his way out.

Hopefully we will not get lost at our parties tomorrow! I don't know all the details, but I know there will be one here at the hospital and one at our house. And apparently this is not some fancy, invitation only type of party because Mom and Dad said I could invite all my friends and they should tell all their friends and their friends to join us.

Now I wish I could tell you these parties were to announce my homecoming, but that is not the theme of these parties. That party will be soon enough. I guess in a way, these parties are to help get us to that party. We can call them the pre-party. See, these parties will be parties where we all come together and pray. Pray that things will go better here in the NICU for me and all my buddies.

I would not be telling the truth if I did not say that things have been rough here recently. Just yesterday I felt lost like my Dad was at his college parties. It was scary. It felt like I was walking through a dark, creepy forest hidden between big mountains that blocked the light. I think it is called a valley. I could not keep myself from walking deeper into this valley and the deeper I got, the darker it got. But as I stood there cold and afraid and alone, the strangest thing happened. The sun shone over the tops of those mountains. It was tiny at first, but then it got brighter and brighter.

As it got brighter, I heard the smallest voice, almost like a whisper, coming from Daddy. I knew that voice even if it was a whisper. It was his praying voice. And the more he prayed, the brighter the light became. And before too long, this light shone so bright, that the darkness could not take it and it had to leave. This light completely overtook the dark shadow that was trying to pull me deeper into the valley.

After all this was over, Daddy told me that what I saw was in fact the sun, however, it was a different kind of sun. He said with this sun you actually have to complete the u to spell it correctly and that it should look something like, Son. Now I do not know what all that means and it seems a little deep for me, but maybe when I am bigger, one of you will explain it to me. All I know is that when I needed some Light to drive away this dark shadow, it came. You can spell it anyway you want, but I know it was real.

As I drift off to sleep tonight in the warmth of the Light, know that I will pray that whatever dark and lonely and scary valley you might find yourself in, that the same Light that led me and Daddy out of our dark places will guide you.

I love being your buddy!

> *"Even though I walk through the darkest valley,*
> *I will fear no evil, for you are with me."*
> (Psalms 23:4, NIV)

CHAPTER THIRTY-FIVE
Old Friends

My mind circled back to the day when our doctor told us she could not save both Erin and Faith, when she warned us that there was a zero percent chance our baby would live.

Now there I was, sitting in my wonderfully worn leather chair, warming my face by a fire and experiencing such deep contentment. The prayer meetings with our friends were perfect, and neither Erin nor I had words that could've contained the immense gratitude we held in our hearts for the support and care we received. But the security I basked in at that moment wasn't from the meetings. It had come in a more intimate way when it was just me and God sitting in the hospital chapel waiting for everyone to arrive.

As had happened the night before when I'd first stepped into that timeless chapel, my heart had been racing a bit, like an athlete before a big game. I'd paced for a bit, making quick circular laps around the small chapel. But the mood of the room was too strong of an influence as it turned my laps into a contemplative stroll. Eventually I surrendered my anxiety to the tangible peace of the space, and, thankful there were still many minutes before others showed up, I sank into a pew, cherishing the solitude.

Closing my eyes, I breathed in the presence of God. My thoughts swirled back in time, reliving the previous day when I'd stood hopelessly as Faith had slipped away from us. Don't get me wrong, God, I'm so, so, so thankful You saved her life, but what was that all about? I was so scared, and I felt so helpless...please help me make sense out of all of this. Please help me understand what You are doing? Help me see what You see.

Silence.

Except for the honey-infused light beams around me, there was nothingness.

Until...until the nothingness morphed into something-ness, and the something-ness began to feel like everything-ness, as if

God was wrapping His arms around me.

A warmth I had experienced so often in times of prayer settled on my shoulders and melted throughout my being. Then it covered me until it eventually filled every dark and empty crack inside of me. At that moment, something shifted. The tectonic plates of my soul adjusted into a firmer foundation. Every question I had ever asked, as well as every one I was too afraid to ask, was satisfied in an unexplainable way. I did not have the answers or solutions about how to ensure that Faith would live, but I possessed something better than that: an indescribable, supernatural peace in my heart. A deep knowing that if her eyes never opened on this side of heaven, her first view would be of something much more precious than this world. She would see another world, another realm, and even more glorious, her eyes' first gaze would be upon Jesus. The thought sucked my breath from my chest just imagining what that glory would feel like.

Even if Faith was called home much earlier than Erin or I wanted, she would not be just okay; she would be more than okay. She would be whole. Healed. Filled. And I knew that even in the seemingly bottomless hole of grief and despair, Erin and I would also be comforted. And healed. And filled, by the very spirit and heart of our Father God. He, too, knew the depths of pain of losing a child, and He was more than equipped to carry us through to hope.

My eyes once again met the chapel painting of Jesus teaching the Beatitudes, and the words *"Blessed are those who mourn, for they will be comforted"* etched themselves deeply into my heart. While God didn't answer the original questions, He had offered the answers I truly needed, the ones that brought transformation to my soul.

As I sat now in my leather armchair, I thanked God that the strength He had infused me with in the chapel was still with me tonight, hanging around like an old friend that you never want to leave.

CHAPTER THIRTY-SIX

Skin to Skin

Days went by and Faith's lungs did not improve. She still needed the ventilator, the oxygen saturation levels were still too high, and she was still not thriving. Nothing had changed. And yet everything had changed. Dread was no longer my daily companion, and my inner strength had divorced itself from outward circumstances; no matter what the report or status was on Faith's health, hope and peace held my heart up and kept me believing that no matter what, we were going to be okay.

"I think I'm finally getting it," I said to Erin over morning coffee. We had been sitting and chatting and laughing like the days before we knew the meanings of medical terms like placenta abruption, apnea, and bradycardia. This normalcy had been hibernating, tucked away somewhere hoping springtime would usher in a revival. But we had found it again, well before spring, and we were both so grateful. It was so good to sit with my wife again, both of us genuinely joyful.

"What do you mean?" she asked.

"Well, from the very beginning of all of this, you've been walking in a kind of supernatural spiritual rain suit that seems to protect you from the storm ranging around us. You got your word from God, and you've been unshakable. Me, on the other hand...I feel like I've been drenched in this storm, clothed only in my underwear."

"I get that my faith swings have been worse than the mood swings of a pre-teen girl—but I feel like I've finally got it."

"Got what?"

"What you have. Faith that doesn't move even when circumstances do. It's like I'm walking in this dual truth. On one hand, our daughter is not improving, we are running out of options, and there is sadness and pain in knowing that. On the other hand, I feel this joy and peace"—I searched to find the right words—"like God has breathed hope over those scary emotions and truths and that hope is so much stronger than anything that could happen. Is any of this making sense?"

Erin reached over and took my hand. "Yes. That's exactly it. It's like the two truths are walking side by side. Only one is much bigger than the other and it has taken the smaller one by the hand to make sure it can't run around like a crazy person."

"Yeah, I've definitely felt like that crazy person," I commented, to which Erin agreed.

"That is a good point. You were running in the dark, in the rain, dressed in a suit."

"Well"—I sprung up and stepped toward the sink to rinse out my coffee cup—"in the spirit of always including you in both my ups and my downs, let me show you what that run was like." And I dashed her with the cold-water sprayer.

Screaming with surprise, she popped up with her water bottle, and the kitchen water fight commenced. We played and laughed and drenched each other. Our old selves had been completely released from their hibernation, and I almost cried from the joy of it all.

After we dried off and cleaned up, we drove together to the hospital to visit and pray over our baby girl. It was one of those late winter days in Birmingham when spring had burst through with its bright sun and unseasonably warm temperatures. The gorgeous beauty of the morning was so perfect as we walked toward the entrance that when I saw Jack sitting outside on a bench, he seemed out of place. His slouched body language did not match the sparkle of the sun, and it compelled to see what was wrong.

"You go on ahead." I motioned toward the bench. "I'm going to talk to Jack."

Sitting next to Jack, I waited until he looked up to speak.

"Hey there." I put my hand on his shoulder. "How are y'all doing?"

Sighing deeply, Jack responded. "You know as well as anyone, Blake, there are good days, and there are misguided days. These past several...well...we've had a string of them."

"Man, I am so sorry to hear that. But I know exactly what you mean. Sometimes I feel like the guide for our days has quit. How's Ainsley?"

"She's good. Honestly, my wife amazes me with her grit."

Ain't that the truth.

"Jack, you're not alone. Can I tell you something that happened to me the past few days that has really changed my perspective?"

"Please. I'd love to hear."

I shared everything with Jack. The fears I'd had, the struggles with the unknown, the day in the chapel, the power of our prayer meetings, and how God had infused me with a deep hope. With every word, I watched as God used my story to breathe life back into Jack's soul. We prayed together, maybe shed a few man tears together, and left each other the better for it.

Every time I had ever been with Jack, I'd left his company uplifted; it felt so great to have returned the favor to this mighty man of faith. Another reminder that the act of giving is never a loss for the giver. Whether it's time or money or knowledge or energy or love, when we give of ourselves, we walk away richer than if we'd kept it all for ourselves.

When I arrived at the NICU, Erin was perched over our daughter singing a hymn. Would this little baby ever grasp what this incredible woman had done for her, had risked for her? Erin had placed her life in the gap so that Faith might live, and my heart burned for Faith to grow up and tell this story. I snuck up behind my wife and gave her a hug.

"How are y'all doing?" The nurse stepped in to check on Faith. "Our little girl gave us some fits this morning, but right now she seems to be doing just fine, thank God."

As she continued her routine of checks, I noticed Erin watching the nurse. She was on the edge of her seat with an expression I knew well. She was about to ask for something big, and honestly, I felt a bit of trepidation for whatever was going to come spilling, unchecked, out of my wife's mouth. Either way, a moment of truth was coming.

"Do you think I could hold her?" Erin asked quietly, but with the confidence of a mama lion.

Both the nurse and I shot each other glances of uncertainty. While in a normal scenario, a mom asking permission to hold her own baby would seem strange, in the NICU world, this was the status quo. Very small and early babies are guarded from receiving too much stimulation as even the smallest of touches could impact their heart rates, their ability to breathe, and even their development. The nurse's expression wavered from professional to personal. I wondered if she was a mom herself. If so, she would fully comprehend the agony a mother experiences forced to watch her baby struggle inside a plastic box and suppress the fierce instinct to gather her child close to her chest.

"Have you ever gotten to hold her?" she asked Erin.

Erin's eyes misted as she answered, "No."

This nurse was definitely a mother. Her own eyes filled with tears and a resolve fixed on her face. She understood. And perhaps she also knew the gravity, the reason why Erin was asking what she was asking. Erin's request was not an off-the-cuff question. It came from the primal place inside a woman that screams out, I must protect my baby against any wicked thing that threatens. The place that vows to never rest until she squelches all the lurking dangers. The place that stays put and carries on, even when the father is not man enough to stay.

But Erin's request also came from the unspoken reality that she knew and I knew and the nurse definitely knew, there might not be many more opportunities to hold her baby.

"Today is your day, Mama." The nurse spoke with a tight voice, holding back emotion.

Because germs could be on her shirt, in what seemed an instant, Erin was sitting topless in the chair beside Faith's box, intently zoned in on the nurse's instructions. Also, Erin cherished the skin-to-skin connection that comes from the miracle of nursing, and until this point, she'd been robbed of this experience. As the nurse removed the top of Faith's box, we all sensed the holy moment about to occur and our voices shifted to whispers of awe.

Silence and wonder pervaded as the nurse placed Faith's tiny body on Erin's bare chest, their skin touching for the very first time. Was it just my imagination that a radiant beam simultaneously swirled out from the sound of their heartbeats, once again beating side-by-side, engulfing them in stunning beauty? It was as it should be. As it should have been. For at least another ten weeks, these heartbeats should have been rhythmically intertwined in utero as Faith grew to full term. Perhaps this magical connection would be the elixir for Faith's lungs to finally obey the command of their mother? For Faith's little body to respond and to mature, and more importantly, to live?

As my eyes were drenched in tears, I was curious why Erin did not cry. But I understood. Feeling the almost weightlessness of Faith's tiny body resting on her chest was a moment to be cherished and taken in completely. There was no room to waste even one ounce of energy on anything except this intimacy between Mama and her baby, a brief moment that might need to hold a lifetime worth of living.

CHAPTER THIRTY-SEVEN

Home

Sometimes they say home is where you hang your hat or home is where your heart is. While both things may be true, I'm not sure either goes deep enough to point to our true home. Right now, for me, my true home is with my mommy in her tummy. But I can't be there. I guess sometimes the place you have to live in is not the home that you had hoped for. Where you are might not even be the home you are supposed to be in, but you have to make the best of it. You might even have been told to leave the home you so desperately wanted to live in or worked so hard to create. I can relate. Doctors had to cut me out of my perfect little home!

So, why am I talking about all this home stuff? Because I got to go home today!

Oh wait...when I say 'home' it might mean something different to me than it does to you. I didn't get to go to my home where my mommy and daddy and sister live; that's still a long time away. I have a lot more growing to do before I get to do that. When I say 'home' I mean the only home I've ever known. Ever since I've been out in this big, bright world, I haven't been able to go where I belong. But when I got to go there tonight, I can't even tell you how happy it made me. I had forgotten how much I'd missed it, how much I needed it, until I was there.

Home for me is my mommy. I got to lie on her chest and feel her warm skin and the vibrations when she spoke. But maybe my favorite thing is that I got to listen to the very familiar sound of her heartbeat. In her arms, I was home, and I never wanted to leave that safe and wonderful place. While she held me, I tried my very, very best to keep breathing because I had a feeling if my lungs stopped working, I would have to go back to my box.

All this talk of home got me thinking about how there are probably a lot of us who live somewhere that we never thought we would call home. Maybe you are like me and the home that you thought was perfectly made for you was whisked away. Maybe someone told you that you could no longer stay in your home. Maybe you did everything right or maybe you did some things wrong, but either way, you are now fighting to survive in a place that seems so strange and scary and lonely that you find it hard to breathe sometimes. You even sometimes feel like your heart stops beating. Well, our circumstance might be a little different, but believe me when I say, I can relate.

I had a home that was so nice and warm and protected. A place that was built by God Himself. And then one day, out of the blue, that home was taken from me. And now I find myself in a place that is cold and lonely, and I sometimes feel like I am suffocating and then other times my heart literally stops beating. If I am being honest, I find it all very scary, confusing, and just plain unfair. All I want is to be back with my family, tucked safely in Mommy's tummy, but that seems so far away it is hard to see it from here. And if I was being real honest, I would have to admit that I am not sure that I am ever even going to make it out of here.

But when I feel like I can't go on anymore, I think about something my daddy told me during one of his late-night visits. I did not fully understand it, but he was talking in his praying voice, and I could feel something different and new and alive wrapping around me. It was like home was coming to me, even though home seemed to be so far away. He said something about Jesus living in an unfamiliar land. He talked about how Jesus left a home that was perfect and arrived here in this world in a scary situation, just like I did. Daddy talked about how Jesus's future probably seemed uncertain. He asked Jesus to give him the same strength and perspective that He had. The perspective that kept Jesus moving forward, even when the way forward was so hard. Then Daddy ended that prayer by saying that Jesus endured His struggles because of a hope that was set before Him and that Daddy needed to have that same hope.

I don't know a lot about this world, or Jesus, or really much of anything when I think about it, but I know I felt something when Daddy talked about hope. It was like Jesus and Daddy were building a home around me. It felt so strange and familiar at the same time. I knew I was not in the home I was supposed to be in, but I also felt that Jesus was not concerned about that, and He was going to make a home for me right where I was.

Times still get hard, but when they do, I try to think about that hope Daddy talked about, and that home Jesus is making for me.

So as I snuggle my tiny self into my bedsheets tonight, I am going to picture me and you and Jesus sitting by a nice warm fire, our toes covered in a warm blanket, and drinking hot chocolate while we talk and laugh and play games. Who knows, maybe that was the hope that helped Jesus overcome His hard days.

"My Father's house has many rooms; if that were not so, would I have told you that I am going there to prepare a place for you? And if I go and prepare a place for you, I will come back and take you to be with me that you also may be where I am."

John 14:2–3, NIV

CHAPTER THIRTY-EIGHT

Legacy

As I pecked mindlessly at numbers on a spreadsheet, I found it difficult to focus. On a normal day at the office, diving into a clean spreadsheet to strategize and study a client's situation revitalized me. On a normal day, I had confidence in my ability to solve any situation or problem with numbers as my tools and my mind as the engine. But today was not a normal day. Who was I kidding? We hadn't had one of those since the end of last summer.

I had stopped in early to visit Faith before work, and she was not doing well at all. I'd have gladly taken a normal day of Faith moderately struggling to breathe over this morning's abnormal day of her sats going in all the wrong directions. After I'd left, I called Erin, just to share with her how troubled I was with Faith's lack of progress. I'd expected to hear her usually undaunted optimism, but this time she'd simply agreed with me. And attempting to drown out my concern with spreadsheets and numbers was not working.

About 10:30, my cell rang with a call from the hospital. The urge to bolt outside and never come back almost got the better of me. If I didn't answer, then nothing bad could happen. But I also could not not know what they had to tell me.

"This is Blake," I answered.

"Blake, Dr. Armando here." His voice sounded heavy. Maybe I should've run when I'd had the chance. "Is this a good time to talk?"

"Sure."

"I know you visited Faith this morning, and you must know she is not doing well. We cannot seem to get her lungs to do what we need them to do. We are currently at 100% on her oxygen, and she still is only in the eighties for her saturation levels."

He paused. Was I supposed to say something? What should I say? Before I could formulate a response, he continued.

"I wanted to call you because I met with our entire team today, as well as consulted with some of the best neonatologists in the area, and we all agree that the best course of action for Faith is to transfer her to UAB. We believe they could do some things for her there that we cannot do for her here."

Irony is not my friend. I couldn't count how many times I'd wondered if Faith would be better off with Dr. Carlo at UAB, but now that the day had come, my heart felt like lead in my chest.

"Dr. Armando." It took effort to keep my voice from cracking. "Faith is more fragile than she has ever been. We can barely touch her. I just don't see how we could safely move her."

"I understand your concern, but we would not recommend it if we did not think it was in her best interest. UAB has a machine called an oscillating ventilator that helps with how the vent delivers oxygen into her lungs. I know you have a good relationship with Dr. Carlo, and I personally talked to him before I called you. He agreed this was the best next step."

"I hear you, I really do, but I'm not sure she can handle the move." My strategic mind tried grasping at a different solution. "Couldn't we borrow the oscillator? I have a truck. I could bring it over."

There was another pause. Was that good? Was he going to take me up on the offer to transport the machine to him?

"Blake, I care about you, but we all feel the best place for Faith is at UAB." I didn't like where this was going. "You need to understand, there is nothing else we can do for Faith."

The finality of the words, "there is nothing else we can do for Faith" burned through my heart like an arrow from the enemy's camp. Shot from some hidden and cowardly place. And it hit dead center.

I had nothing else to offer in the conversation, so I simply said "okay" and hung up. For the second time in as many months, we had been given a death sentence for Faith. I stood at my window and cried.

After several minutes, I pulled myself together enough to call Erin and share the conversation. She responded with a quiet resolve, which didn't surprise me. She said she would handle the details for care of Rebekah so we could both be fully present for the transfer. Next, I called my mom. For reasons yet unknown to me, I felt the need to meet her in person to relay the news. I asked her if she could meet me for coffee at the Starbucks in her neighborhood.

Mom was already there when I arrived, and her expression conveyed she understood there was more than coffee with this impromptu date.

"Hey, son." She greeted me with a hug. "What's going on?"

So much for small talk.

"It's a pretty day, Mom. Let's walk outside."

The sun felt like a giant bucket of glowing life pouring itself over Birmingham. Mom and I walked through the glow long enough to get away from the hustle and bustle of the crowded downtown streets and into a quiet neighborhood. Here the houses stood far from the street, but to be safe, I didn't stop leading my mom until we hit the dead end of a cul-de-sac. Only there did I feel hidden enough to reveal the news I'd just received and my emotions about it.

"So," I announced, facing her. "Faith is going on a field trip. It seems the Lord has answered our prayers and decided for us. Faith is being transferred to UAB."

"Okay," she answered. "What does that mean? What do you need from me?"

Mom, always the practical one, needed every detail. I relayed the full conversation I'd had with Dr. Armando, and the entire time, I felt split in half. One half was relaying words to my mother, and the other was wildly searching my soul, attempting to process the storm clouds churning in my gut. A tornado was rising, and I had no idea how to bridle it. After I had answered all her questions, I began to pace.

"Son," my mom whispered. "Please let me help you."

"Why is this happening?!" I hurled words at her, at God, at the injustice.

"Why is what happening?" Her voice treaded softly.

The tornado erupted. Loudly.

"Why is Faith dying?! Why? Can you tell me that? Because I do not understand why we had to come so far, all the way to this point, only to have her die!" My head was swirling with rage. "Why couldn't God have just taken her back in December? Or, back in September when all of this started?! What kind of sick joke is it for us to go through all of this emotional torture?"

Realizing my vocal levels were reaching a near shout, I took a few breaths before going on.

"He led us to do this CaringBridge site and people are following us now, getting encouraged...they connected with what I thought God was saying through it, and now what? We're just going to get on there and let everyone know that Faith died? That after all this time of getting on our knees and praying that she did not make it? That God actually decided to not answer our prayers? What was the point of all this? What was the purpose?"

I felt like I'd uncorked a rush of feelings that were now impossible to bottle back up. Maybe I should've gone for a run instead. My legs itched to sprint. But I was stuck with my mom, forced to face the words I'd just spewed.

"Oh, my son," Mom finally said. "I know you are hurting so badly right now. I wish there was something I could do to make this pain stop for you. To make it stop for Faith." She took a moment before she added, "You are wrestling with the purpose, and that is completely understandable. I would be, too. But could I ask you a few questions about that?"

I wasn't sure I wanted to continue this painful conversation, but I nodded.

"You mentioned the CaringBridge site. How many people do you think that site has reached? Not just the ones who commented, but all the churches and prayer groups they represent?"

"I don't know, Mom."

"Just estimate. How many people?"

"It would be so difficult to measure that...three hundred? Maybe more?"

"So, would you say the site has encouraged these three hundred people? That they've been given a small picture of who God is?"

"Yes, and that is exactly my point." I felt the heat rising again. "All these people saw a picture of God, and now that Faith is dying, they are going to see a picture of the God who strings you along only to let your dreams fall apart. How is that helpful? It would have been better to not have included them in our journey at all!"

"Blake, do you really think God's ultimate goal for us is to make everything work out the way we want it?"

"No," I said, frustrated. "No, I don't think that. I know that sometimes on this broken earth, we face terrible circumstances. But in our case, I just don't understand why He had to let His 'ultimate plan' play out in such a public and painful way. Why could Faith not have just gone on to be with Him months ago, quietly and peacefully? Why did she have to suffer for all these weeks?" Frustration shifted to heartbreak as I imagined the pain my baby had been enduring. "Why did she have to hurt so much?"

With my frustration overwhelming me, I sank to the ground. My mom sat beside me and held my hand, then my head, and eventually wrapped her arms completely around me. We sat there at the edge of some stranger's driveway, crying together underneath the glowing sunshine that was pouring out over Birmingham. When the tears finally stopped, my mom picked up the conversation.

"Blake, what do you think is the meaning of life?"

"Mom. Can we maybe try to unpack the Top 10 list of life's greatest questions another time? We're sitting on someone else's property."

"They're at work," she said, unfazed. "I'm serious. What do you think this is all about? What would you say is a good legacy? After all your days are done, how would you like your life to be measured?"

"I don't know." I sucked in a deep sigh. "I guess I would want people to say I was a good man. That I'd stayed true to my wife and raised my kids well. That I was a good friend. That I'd made a difference in my community, somehow helped make people's lives better. Helped them connect with Jesus."

"I would agree with you," she said. "I'd say those are all things that would leave a meaningful legacy, that would help make other's lives better. So let me ask you this: Do you think Faith has made a difference in the lives of those around her? During the time she has had on this earth, has Faith been a blessing to others? What about those three hundred people that have visited her CaringBridge pages? Has she blessed them?"

"Yes." Beginning to understand where she was going with this, my heart lifted. "I would guess that they probably have."

"Do you think they would have been able to feel what they felt, to experience what they experienced, if Faith had been taken home back in September?"

My eyes stung with tears. "No," I whispered. "No, I don't."

"I don't either." My mom smiled. "Son, I believe God works in mysterious ways and that He can see so much that we can never see. He looks down on all of us as His precious children and longs to help us experience the life He desperately wants us to have. A life built on Him and a life built by Him. And many times, He uses us to help each other discover this life."

I exhaled. Somehow Mom always knew what to say.

"Blake, your dad and I have watched you and Erin choose to believe in something you could not see. You both were told your baby had a zero percent chance to live, but you believed that something bigger was possible, and out of that came our precious Faith. Do you understand how many people's lives were impacted simply by that example? Then she, in turn, has touched so many people from her humble and challenging existence that she has been asked to live up to this point. And most of that is because you and Erin have allowed Faith to have a voice. Through the CaringBridge site, and how you've lived through this, you've given that tiny life a voice to speak loudly about the goodness of God."

As she spoke, my heart slowed. Every word she offered brought comfort, and I was grateful to have such a wonderful, compassionate mother. The kind who would sit and cry with me in broad daylight, without worrying one bit about what anyone who might see us would think.

"I don't know what is going to happen to Faith from here. I wish I could pray enough, believe enough, pay enough to make all her hurts go away and all her troubles disappear. But I can't. And you can't. And UAB can't, and Dr. Carlo can't. But what I do know is that Faith's life has been important. No matter how short or long it may be, her life has served and is serving a purpose. It has meaning. Faith's life has brightened the days and nights of so many people."

I squeezed her hand and let each word sink in.

After a long pause, Mom continued, perhaps sensing I needed to hear the message one more time. "None of us are promised tomorrow, but we do have today, and while Faith has today, you and Erin have allowed her to use it in the best way you knew how. And even if Faith does go home to be with the Lord, she will go with a legacy that says, "I used what very little I had to do the best I could to find a way to make a difference in the lives of those people around me." And I think if Faith could stand up and add a closing statement to that legacy she would say, "That was enough."

"Mom, I know you are right. But what else can I do for Faith? How can I help her? I feel so lost and helpless."

"Son, you are already doing it."

"What does that mean? I am not sure I feel like figuring out some philosophical riddle."

"I know you want to help Faith. To do something to make her pain go away. To put her in a better place. To make sure she lives. But so often we are just not able to provide those solutions. Life just won't allow it. But what you can do, what you are doing, is stand firm. You and Erin have not run away from the pain. You have not turned from the hard things. You have stood firm and by simply standing you have given Faith the best possible platform life can offer her right now."

"If you are looking for what you need to do, you just need to keep standing. Don't let the weight of reality push you too far down."

As I sat awkwardly in this stranger's driveway, I again realized that God was doing something so much bigger than I could have ever dreamed of. Listening to Mom speak had brought back the sustaining wind of hope that had propelled my soul since that day in the chapel.

Walking together back to our cars, I felt like I was once and for all starting to realize that all was not lost. There was a purpose to all the twists and turns that had led us to this point. And even if the unimaginable did end up becoming reality, I could lay my head down at night and look through the tears of pain and loss and see something off in the distance. Something that I had been searching so hard for these last several months. Maybe I'd been searching for it most of my life.

I would look through those tears and see meaning. I would look through that pain and see others. I would look through the loss and see purpose. God's purpose. I would know that sometimes the best, and hardest, thing I can do is to just stand firm. And, as my mother had reminded me, that was enough.

CHAPTER THIRTY-NINE

Poker

I've always wondered how Jochebed, Moses's mother, had the courage to make a homemade basket, drop in her baby son whom she'd risked her life for, and then push it off into the Nile River, one famous for being riddled with crocodiles? What kind of crazy person does that? Or maybe it was her crazy faith? Or maybe, out of utter desperation, the only way to save Moses's life was to risk it by launching him into the dangerous waters? The rest, she must have believed, was in God's hands.

As Erin and I allowed strangers to carry our daughter away in the ambulance, we felt like Jochebed, and I understood a little better that mother's desperate act.

Erin and I knew Faith was in such a fragile state that even the brief trip from one hospital to another could be her death sentence. But, like Jochebed, we had little choice. The only way to save Faith's life was to risk it, to allow the ambulance to transfer her, and the rest was in God's hands.

Walking to Faith's new NICU room at UAB, I again experienced a dual truth. Half of me wanted to sprint madly to find out how she had faired in the commute, and the other half wanted to cement my feet to the ground and never know. The agony of not knowing was more terrifying than knowing the worst had happened, and the thought propelled me down the hall.

My heart was beating out of my chest when I entered Faith's room, where Erin was already waiting. No way would she allow Faith to arrive to an empty space. My eyes dove deeply into hers, hoping to read the emotions that would surely communicate the state of our daughter. No tears, no sorrow. I breathed a sigh of relief.

"Hello, Mr. Hamby!" Dr. Carlo greeted. "Faith has made the trip well. We've situated her in her new bed, and she is resting."

Faith looked dead. Completely still. Dr. Carlo sensed my concern and added, "We needed to sedate her for the trip, which was a good thing. Don't worry, she will come out of that medication soon. Here, let me explain the new ventilator she is on."

After he described the advantages of the oscillating ventilator and how it would help Faith, he continued to explain what we could expect over the next several weeks. He emanated such pride, like a master of ceremonies touring us through the aspects of the show we were about to experience, all the doctors and nurses we'd be working with, the design of the private room that included a couch/bed, a shower, and shelving for us to store our things. After our curtained Area 5 with one rolling chair and a Saran-wrapped box, this was like checking into the Ritz.

Thirty minutes flew by as he answered every question I thought I would ever have, and just in case more came to mind, he reminded me I had his cell number to use at any time. The grace and comfort he extended was so overwhelming, I had to fight off the urge to either tip him generously or salute him.

The three Hambys then sat in silence. Sometimes words are unable to carry the weight of the moment. Erin and I, hand in hand, watched over our tiny baby in her new box.

About an hour later, a team of doctors quietly entered our room. UAB is a teaching hospital, so interns and medical professionals usually flank the doctors and nurses. Taking the lead, a tall man with a salt and pepper beard who looked like his second job was appearing in Yeti commercials spoke up. How he sat in front of us, with all these interns standing behind him, and still made us feel like we were the only ones in the room impressed me. He shared much of what Dr. Carlo had explained, but also the many details about the specific medical strategies he felt would help Faith, along with the many potential side effects. Erin's hand around mine tightened proportionally with each strategy until I held up my hand to stop him.

"If you don't mind, let me jump in." I looked over at Faith. There was a pause in the room as I sensed everyone's eyes followed suit. My eyes held my baby girl as I spoke. "When I was in college, I played more poker than I care to let my parents know about. So many times, closer to morning than night, I'd sit around an old wooden table in my fraternity house, with most of my chips gone, and I knew there was not enough time to scrape my way back. The only thing to do was push all my chips out there and go all in." My eyes met my wife's, and they shone with the same mist in mine.

"That's where we are. We get that without a miracle, we are out of chips." My voice cracked with emotion, and I took a moment to clear my throat. "Sir, we appreciate very much and respect all you are trying to communicate to us, but I already know our answer to whatever strategy or means you think might be a good course of action. If you have something, anything, you believe has the remote possibility of helping our daughter, then please do it.

You have our permission."

My words hung in the room as he looked at us with a knowing that we understood the full reality of our situation, that Faith might not make it much longer on this earth. His kindness reached out from his eyes.

"I understand," he said. "And I can promise you we will do whatever we can for your daughter."

After the last few very intense hours, we needed a change of scenery and some fresh air. "How about we go to Moe's?" I asked. Erin nodded. Once inside the restaurant, we found our way to a table in the back corner, away from everyone else.

Erin's words were still locked up inside her head, so I leaned back in my chair and allowed my own thoughts to gather. After several minutes, each of us alone in our thoughts, I threw out a bridge to connect us.

"So, what do you think?" I asked. Okay, maybe that was too big of a bridge to toss out before Erin had even had a chance to take her first bite of burrito.

With dark and hollow eyes, she answered, "I think this sucks."

There was no denying that, so I thought it best to hold my

words for the time being. I wanted to tell her about my conversation with my mom, how I had at last gripped a hold of the clarity and the purpose of all this. How I felt more centered than ever before. But Erin was in a different space, one I had never seen her in from the moment she heard God speak to her and call our baby "Faith." Her feet were always the ones firmly rooted in the courage and security of those words while I'd vacillated. There would be time later for the words of courage. What I needed to do right now was to extend her the same sensitivity she'd always offered to me, and to take the steps across the bridge to meet her where she was at.

"Erin, I love you," I said. "More than I know how to express. Whatever comes, we will walk through it together. God will carry us, and we will be okay."

We finished our food with few words in between bites.

The chill greeted us as we walked back to UAB. Erin stopped walking and when I turned around, her eyes were pleading with the words she couldn't seem to speak.

"What is it?" I asked.

Her wild eyes were filled with sorrow, as she simply said, "I don't want my baby to die."

She melted in my arms, and, despite the cold weather, I stood holding her under a sole streetlamp on an empty pathway. Words wouldn't have helped bring consolation, so we simply embraced until this wave of tears had run dry.

Back inside the warmth of Faith's new NICU suite, the cold reality of her condition stood strong. The ventilator was still pumping 100% oxygen, her saturation levels were still only 80%, and she still lay motionless inside her incubator. Erin and I sat on the couch while I logged on to our CaringBridge site to let everyone know we had lived through the transfer. By the time I'd finished a quick post, the weight of the day had taken its toll and I was ready for my bed. Packing up my laptop to leave, I noticed Erin was not moving.

"Are you not ready to leave yet?" I asked. "I was hoping to get home and spend a little time with Rebekah before we crashed."

"I'm not going home." Her voice was just above a raspy whisper.

"But you don't have anything to change into." I nodded toward the empty wardrobe. "Why don't you come home and get some rest? Then you can stay tomorrow night when you're more prepared."

"I'm staying tonight." The finality of her words matched her expression. It was the same look she gave when the doctor told us there was a zero percent chance Faith would make it. If that look could speak, it would've said, "Not on my watch." Only tonight, this expression had a footnote: "But if something is going to happen on my watch, then I'm going to be right here as it does. My baby will not enter into the arms of her heavenly Father alone."

After a long embrace, I slipped out of the room.

CHAPTER FORTY
Sisters

My collar woke me up. Sprawled atop the covers, still in my work clothes from the day before, I scraped enough cognizance together to remember crashing on our bed solo.

8:14. Wow. That's much later than I usually wake up on a weekday. Perhaps my office work could wait another day.

Staggering down the hallway, I found Rebekah and my mom playing with dolls. What would we be doing right now without the constant help of both our sets of parents? My mind was too foggy to express my gratitude at the moment, so I shuffled to the source that would sweep the cobwebs from my brain. Coffee.

No sooner had I sat on the ground next to Rebekah, coffee tumbler sufficiently capped for playtime, than she curled up in my lap. This was one million times better than sitting at my desk.

"This is my favorite doll, Bell." She said, showing me her newest doll. "I give to Faiff when she comes home."

My heart cracked at the innocence of her toddler words. My mom and I shared knowing looks, and I decided to allow the beauty of Rebekah's childlike faith to capture the moment.

"Have you heard from Erin this morning?" Mom whispered.

I shook my head no. Couldn't I just sit here not-knowing and play with my innocent Rebekah curled in my lap? But I knew Erin would expect my call, no matter how much I was dreading hearing the news. Kissing Rebekah on the head, I slipped into the kitchen and out the back door.

"Hey," Erin answered. "I was wondering when you were going to call."

By her tone, I predicted there was an 87% chance Faith was still alive.

"Yeah, I can't believe how late I slept. Can you believe I crashed in my dress clothes? How did you sleep? How is Faith?"

"Well," she sounded tired. "I did not sleep, and Faith is about the same."

I exhaled. Same was better than the alternative. "I'm so sorry you didn't sleep, but I'm glad you got to spend that time with Faith."

"Me, too. It was really good, and honestly, I needed that time." Her voice shifted with the next sentence. "I want to bring Rebekah up here today."

"Uh, I don't think they'll let that happen, will they?"

"I've already asked them." There was that finality again. "It's time for Rebekah to meet her sister."

I didn't need to ask for clarification; I knew why Erin was pushing for this.

The plan was for me to wait with Rebekah in the NICU March of Dimes waiting room until Erin picked us up. Rebekah flitted around, exploring the games, coloring books, and building blocks while I reclined in the living room area with a huge TV. This room felt cleaner, nicer, and more comfortable than a normal waiting room, and I was reminded again about how much difference the small details make. I was thankful for the March of Dimes and how they served so well.

Erin strode straight to Rebekah and swung her into her arms. I could not tell if Rebekah was more excited to see her mom or meet her sister for the first time.

"Rebekah, do you want to meet your sister?" Erin asked.

"Yes, Mommy. Is she here?"

"Of course! She has her own room now, and I got to spend the night with her last night."

Rebekah's eyes popped open, "Mommy, did you sleep in her box wiff her?"

Erin chuckled, "No sweetie, there is a bed for me, too."

"Okay, Mommy, let's go see Faiff now!" Rebekah jumped up and down and skipped the entire way to Faith's room but when she got to Faith's room, she somehow knew to be quiet because she tiptoed in with exaggerated, toddler steps. Her eyes scanned the room.

"Mommy, I no see Faiff?"

"She's over here, Bek. Let me pick you up and show you."

As Erin lifted Rebekah up to see Faith, I wondered if something magical would happen. Maybe there would be some sibling connection that would finally pull Faith out of the doldrums. Or maybe a childlike faith would come over Rebekah, and she would command the spirit of bad lungs to be removed from Faith in Jesus's name. Or maybe, Rebekah would channel her inner Anna and bring an act of true love to thaw the Frozen situation Faith found herself in.

Not surprisingly, none of those things happened. Rebekah only looked at Faith for a second and said, "Mommy, why don't she have her shirt on?"

I smiled at the perfectly legitimate question for a twenty-two-month-old to ask.

For the first time ever, the four Hambys sat alongside each other as a unified tribe. As we spoke in whispers to Rebekah, answering all her questions about her baby sister, I rested in the reality that this was as it should be. The four of us together, as a family.

The doctor with the pink cowgirl boots stepped into our room. My heart leaped as I remembered how, after I'd seen her on my first tour of UAB laughing and joking with the other doctors, I'd prayed that God would somehow work it out for a cowgirl turned doctor with bright boots to care for our child.

"Hello, am I interrupting anything?" Doctor Cowgirl Boots asked, flashing a Texas-sized smile.

All three of us could not help but reciprocate.

"Dose are really pretty boots!" exclaimed Rebekah.

"And who do we have here?" the doctor asked as she squatted to Rebekah's level.

"I'm Rebekah. Who are you?"

"I'm Dr. Jessie." She extended her hand and firmly shook Rebekah's. "It's very nice to meet you. Do you like stickers?"

Out of her pocket, she pulled several sparkly stickers and handed them to Rebekah.

"Fank you!" she said, as she plopped down on the couch to examine each one.

Standing up, Dr. Jessie composed herself and said, "I just wanted to come by and introduce myself. Erin and Blake Hamby, yes?" We all shook hands. "And this is our little rockstar, Faith." Dr. Jessie quickly performed the series of checks that Erin and I had grown so familiar with. During those checks, Faith had one of her little spells. Thankfully Dr. Jessie and the rest of the team who rushed in were able to settle her fairly quickly.

"I don't want to interrupt your family time, Mr. and Mrs. Hamby. But here is my cell number"— Dr. Jessie scribbled it on the whiteboard on the wall. "Please never hesitate to reach out to me if you need anything. We will watch over Faith very closely, but let us know if you have any questions."

As Dr. Jessie's cowgirl boots clopped out of our room, Erin sat next to Rebekah and hugged her.

"Baby girl," said Erin. "Before you go, would you like to pray for your sister?"

My eyes misted at the suggestion, and I pulled out my phone to record this moment.

Erin picked Rebekah up and walked her to Faith's box. As Erin held Rebekah close, Rebekah looked down on Faith and said, "Faiff, I am glad you are my sister. I want you to come home and play wiff me. Jesus, I know you like little kids because my Bible talks about You playing wiff us. So I need You to make my Faiff better so we can play together. And when You do, we will let You come play wiff us because we know You would like it. Amen."

Rebekah nodded her head as if to say, "So there." And then she asked, "Mommy, do you fink Jesus heard me?"

"I know He did," Erin answered.

CHAPTER FORTY-ONE

Lost

Oh my goodness, oh my goodness! Guess what, guess what! Today was the Best. Day. Ever! I got to meet my big sister, Rebekah, for the first time! She was so much bigger than me. I just know we are going to be the best of sisters and friends once I get outta here.

Actually our visit was so exciting that during the middle of it I had one of those awful spells where my lungs majorly disobey and every alarm started to go off. Nurses piled in as they did everything they knew to do, but my oxygen levels kept hanging out in the low sixties. Eventually, they got me all settled down, and while all that commotion is never fun, the worst part was that it interrupted my playtime with my sister.

And I guess Rebekah was not that interested in all that commotion because at some point, she just up and walked out into the hall. Since Mom was focused on me, she did not realize Rebekah was gone. Well, I don't know what happened while Rebekah was out exploring, but it must have not been as fun as she thought, because at some point she started crying. When she started crying for Mommy, Mommy immediately left me and went to find Rebekah. I guess that is just one of the superpowers that Mommy's have because there sure was a lot of commotion, and I don't know how in the world she heard Rebekah crying for her over all the noise they were making around me. Oh well, however she heard her, I was sure glad she did because after all the fuss over me settled down, Rebekah was back in my room to play with me.

After my family left, I had the room all to myself and was thinking about how wonderful it was to see my sister Rebekah for the first time. I also thought how scary that must have been for her when she realized she did not know where she was and looked around and could not see Mommy or Daddy. I can relate. So many times I have had to look at the scary things around me, with all their scary sounds, and most of the time I don't see Mommy and Daddy either.

But the more I laid here in my box, all by myself, I realized that even when I can't see my parents in the room, I can still feel them in the room. It's kind of weird to say, but maybe they have invisible superpowers because I almost feel like they are with me, even when they are not with me.

I wonder if that is how God is too. Maybe God is

like Mom and has superpowers to allow Him to hear our cries over the noise and chaos that is around us. And maybe, He has invisible superpowers too and is there, even when we can't see that He is there. I wonder if I stopped trying to look so hard with my eyes if I might see Him a little better? Maybe I will work on my superpowers and just close my eyes and see if I might see Him a little clearer then?

> *"The waters closed over my head, and I thought I was about to perish. I called on your name, Lord, from the depths of the pit. You heard my plea: 'Do not close your ears to my cry for relief.' You came near when I called you, and said, 'Do not fear.' You, Lord, took up my case; you redeemed my life."*
>
> Lamentations 3:54–58

CHAPTER FORTY-TWO

Hope

The shuffling of my dress shoes across the office parking lot reflected how exhausted I felt after a long Friday of work. Again I had to fight the urge to drive my truck straight to a happy hour somewhere to get lost in a cold beer and mindless conversation about whatever had happened in the sports world earlier in the week. Instead my hands robotically steered my truck to the UAB NICU. I walked into what had been Faith's room for a week now, and my heart sank when I saw Faith's incubator surrounded by Dr. Carlo and Dr.

Jessie. Had something happened to call them both here?

"Hello, Dr. Carlo." My voice dripped with fear. "Dr. Jessie. Good to see you both. How is our girl doing?"

"Oh, she is doing very well, umm hmm." Dr. Carlo smiled broadly. "Faith's had a really wonderful day."

"I'm glad to hear that," I answered robotically.

As much as I respected Dr. Carlo, I lumped my initial feeling about what he had said into my perception of him as the perfect master of ceremonies. Always positive and encouraging, even if he knew the show would not be as good as others. But as I read Faith's oxygen settings, my robotic heart sparked a bit. Her sats were good. Huh. Maybe our master of ceremonies was not just trying to cheer me up.

"Oh," I added sheepishly. "I see you are being serious. Her vent settings are down, and her oxygen saturation level is up. That is positive, right?"

"Oh yes," Dr. Jessie chimed in. "Very positive."

My heart leaped. "How long has she been on these settings?"

"About three hours," Dr. Carlo said proudly.

"Excuse me?" I had to confirm his words. After such a dark valley, the report seemed destine to slip back down into the dark valley, no matter how many attempts I made to grasp the good news. "Did you really say three hours?"

Both doctors nodded.

"Our tiny girl is really holding strong. In fact..." Dr. Carlo looked at Dr. Jessie. "I think we should turn her vent settings down even further. Let's test and see just where Faith is."

As he walked over to the ventilator settings, I panicked. "Wait. Are you sure? Shouldn't we wait longer to make sure she is ready? What if something happens, and she can't handle it?"

"We'll be right here," Dr. Jessie reassured.

I'm not sure I breathed as Dr. Carlo turned the setting down to 80%.

We stood stoically and waited for a response from Faith. Would she be able to hold her own oxygen levels even with the ventilator turned down?

She did! Her levels held steady in the nineties, just as they should be.

After about five minutes, Dr. Carlo had a sparkle in his eye. "How about we try turning it down to 75%?" The three of us were like a trio exploring a new frontier. My heart dared to expect a positive result.

At 75%, Faith held her oxygen saturation levels on her own exactly where they needed to be.

At 70%, Faith still held strong. I felt like the Alabama defensive line watching as the offense took back the lead in the last minutes of a National Championship. The more my face lit up, the more Dr. Carlo's and Dr. Jessie's did too, until joy was flowing freely from us as we watched Faith breathe in a way that did not look like she was drowning.

After about twenty minutes, a few other nurses who had been taking care of us for the past week sensed the joy and stepped into the room to watch. The vibe in the air was as thick with anticipation as any final moments of an SEC nail-biter, and by the time Dr. Carlo had turned the oxygen down to 65%, I realized this was the best kind of happy hour at the end of a cloudy Friday afternoon I ever could've asked for.

My baby was breathing on her own better than she had since her first couple days on earth! I could barely contain myself. I hugged Dr. Carlo three times before he left, and each nurse got at least one hug, and some of the random people walking down the hall found a hand raised for a high five. My legs, which had robotically shuffled me into the NICU, were now filled with so much fire, they started jumping up and down. As I walked around searching for a place to unleash my overflowing excitement, I had to remind them that not every parent here today was having this success.

I walk-ran to the March of Dimes parent room, and after checking all corners to make sure I was alone, my legs erupted with leaps like I just watched an Alabama come-from-behind win in the last seconds of the National Championship. My fingers frantically found Erin's number on the speed dial and the second she answered, I exclaimed, "Our baby is down to 65% oxygen and holding her stats in the nineties!!"

Shouting erupted from our house as Erin praised the Lord and called for Rebekah to join in. The rejoicing was an elation so beautiful and strong. My heart had found a way to keep itself in the game. It had been so long since we'd felt any kind of victory that my heart had forgotten how to soar. But in those moments, I flung off the blanket of cautious optimism and dove deep into the waters of pure belief and freedom.

Once we'd all exhausted ourselves with celebration and ended our phone party, I sank down in a chair to catch my breath. The enormous window in front of me drew me into a view of my city, and I lost myself in the fresh perspective of this wonderful place, so thankful God had placed us at this spot on the planet. He knew the challenges we would face, and He not only graciously built our lives in a community of people who would champion our family during these difficult times, but He also opened a way for Faith to be taken care of by two exceptional NICUs.

My imagination created a montage of the journey we'd been walking. I remembered seeing Erin so many months earlier, when we thought we'd lost the baby the first time. She'd crunched herself up on a chair in her OBGYN's waiting room, staring out a window much like the one I was now, waiting to run tests. Too early to even know if our second would be a boy or a girl, we held hands praying this tiny life would not be extinguished. Even before we'd chosen a name, we fought for her in prayer, knowing God already knew her name. How happy we were when we heard the heartbeat of that little bean, and how innocently we'd left that appointment unaware that the pattern of heavy bleeding and cramping, fears of miscarriage, trips to the ER, and tests to confirm a strong heartbeat would play out over and over again.

Room 307. So much life had condensed into those weeks, my mind grappled to sort out all the memories. There were barren nights as I lay awake on my little couch-turned-bed, worry blanketing my mind as nightmares of Erin dying harassed my imagination. But there was also joy and life found in that room in ways that seemed like strangers in a foreign land, unaware of how they were supposed to act.

Then Room 307 the second time. We believed God gave us that room again to assure us that He had everything under control. Erin had risked her life to keep Faith in her womb as long as possible, and then our baby was born so many weeks premature and whisked away to become a captive inside a Saran-wrapped plastic box with tubes and machines trying to keep her safe instead of her mommy and daddy. When I'd seen Faith for the first time, my fears and relief battled for first place as I gazed upon her tiny frame, barely alive...but alive just the same.

The memory montage sped up to visual after visual. The midnight runs in the rain. The hospital chapel bathed in the light from the stained-glass windows. How broken I was. How held-together God kept me. The frantic runs up and down the stairwells. The time I'd stood and watched as Faith, surrounded by a fighting army of nurses and doctors, almost slipped out of their highly-trained hands into the clutches of death. My fully-suited sprint through the rain and along very populated streets that desperate night.

Faith's journal entries on CaringBridge. How masterfully God had taken what I was accustomed to doing in the safe confines of my private journal and turned that desire to write out my feelings into a platform to bring meaning to our situation. How He had used a simple and, if I was honest, kind of cheesy mode of communication to give Faith a voice.

Erin. The constant pillar of strength and trust in our God. He had given her a word that our baby would be called Faith, and she'd never wavered from that promise. She'd held firm to her belief that if God said it, then He would do it. Even as I often felt like a double-minded man being tossed to and fro from doubt to faith, my wife had served as the ever-solid anchor, pulling me back to solid ground again and again.

Our community of family and friends. In too many instances to count, these loved ones had reached out to us, invested time in us, provided for us, and prayed for us. Their words had delivered hope and life as they infused both Erin and me with their love that sustained us for the journey. When we were weak, they were strong. When we could not see the path forward they carried us from rock to rock. How could we have managed without them? It was a simple answer: we could not have.

There was also the medical staff. Every single one of them loved us and helped us in their own unique ways and gifting. We saw care delivered from the head of a world-renowned NICU to the individual tasked with maintaining a clean environment in our room and so many in between. When the situation was impossible, they provided not just care, but hope. I wondered again, how could we have ever reached this place without each one of them? It was the same simple answer: we could not have.

And the grand finale of my mental montage was Faith. Her strong heart had fought valiantly for life, even when the internal surroundings of Erin's womb were damaged. How in the world could anyone ever think these tiny, unborn lives were not precious and valuable? To be fought for? That even being the least among us in size, they had the capacity to make vast differences in the world? Faith was proof that even before she took a breath, her life had impacted so many others. How I longed to hold her against my chest and father her into adulthood...but even if I never held her this side of heaven, I knew without doubt I had been part of a miracle. I had seen God's hand. And not just God's hand in Faith, but also His hand in the lives of so many other people we'd encountered because of Faith.

I'm uncertain how long I basked in thankfulness and memories, but when I walked to my truck that night, I was not the same man who'd robotically trudged into the UAB NICU hours earlier. My soul had drunk in a hope that had previously seemed out-of-reach, and my heart was girded with peace.

The deepest of sleep surrounded me that evening as Erin and I held each other until morning. And when I awoke, the fresh sense of strength remained. Although I knew the path forward was still very uncertain, that uncertainty felt relegated to its little corner, guarded by something much bigger: Faith.

CHAPTER FORTY-THREE

Even If

The next several weeks continued a cycle of ups and downs, but for the first time in what seemed like an eternity, Faith celebrated more ups than downs. Through my musings, Faith's voice continued to report her progress through posts on the CaringBridge site, and we continued to be amazed at the outpouring of support.

Over the next few weeks, it seemed we were on a new trajectory where nothing could stop us or shake our faith...until the wheels fell off again. Erin was at the hospital, and I was at work, when the news of the baby's death brought us to our knees.

I don't remember the drive to the hospital. One minute I was sitting in my office listening to my wife's voice, and the very next I was running toward her tear-stained face as she sat in Faith's NICU room. Our bodies collided in an embrace as the questions spilled out of my mouth, "How did you hear the news? Did they call you? How are they doing?"

"Sock, they didn't call." Erin's voice sounded tight. "I saw their post on Facebook. Of course, we wouldn't be on their list to call right now...I just wish there were something we could do to help them."

Erin handed me her phone, and I sank into the couch to read a post from a parent that must have been excruciating to pen. Every word of finality would feel like a pierced wound in the heart, bleeding out. Jack and Ainsley's precious Mary Beth had died.

> *Today was a day our family will remember and hold dear for as long as our family sits around tables and recounts the paths we have taken to get us to where we are. Today, our baby girl Mary Beth walked into the arms of Jesus.*
>
> *After a long, long road with so many turns and detours and wonderful stops full of wonderful people along the way, Mary Beth finally arrived at the destination she*

was destined for. That same destination we are all headed for. While our hearts are broken, they are also held so tightly together that it is hard for us to describe the peace that is resonating through every part of who we are.

Some have asked us how we are processing the loss of Mary Beth after such a long road. Some even have whispered, "How do you make sense of something like this happening?" I guess in a way they are asking, what is the point? And we believe it is a fair question. But after traveling this road, we can assure everyone there is a point. There is a way to make sense of this. If we had the opportunity to go back in time, knowing what we know now, and choose whether or not we would say yes to having Mary Beth come into this world, we would say yes every time. While filled with struggle and pain, her life was also overflowing with love and joy and innocence. She was a blessing in every way to every person she met, and we are better off because she was on this earth.

The loss we, as parents, feel is overwhelming. At some moments, the grief seems all-consuming. But we take confidence in knowing that right now God is dancing with our bundle of joy in His arms, and she is finally free to run and breathe and laugh and live. Mary Beth is in our future, and we are holding on to that hope.

> *There are no words that could possibly contain our gratitude for you. Thank you for lifting us up and carrying us through. Thank you for celebrating the highs with us and grieving the lows with us. Your prayers and support have sustained us, and we will forever be in your debt. We love each and every one of you.*

Stunned silence filled the room as Erin and I stared into nothingness, our minds trying to comprehend the news. My gut felt sucker-punched and my thoughts darted furiously around, aimlessly trying to discover some crack in this narrative that could lead to a different outcome. But there was no crack, not even one, only solid ramparts of concrete.

The clopping of cowboy boots broke through our silence. When Dr. Jessie saw both of our solemn gazes, her broad smile melted into an expression of concern. Sensing the gravity in the room, she slipped into a chair next to the couch where Erin and I sat. After several moments, she spoke quietly.

"What's happened?"

Erin and I exchanged glances, searching each other's eyes to find the words. I only found loss and confusion in Erin's, and I'm sure she saw the same in mine.

"There is a couple we met at the other hospital," I began slowly. "Their baby girl, Mary Beth, was several months older than

Faith, but struggled almost constantly. A precious couple. For weeks we got to know them, and we supported each other, and..."

"They are some of the best people you could ever meet." Erin picked up where my words drifted off. "So strong in their faith."

"Unbelievably strong," I added. "No matter how good or bad things were with Mary Beth, Jack and Ainsley seemed always to have this joy...they had no doubt God was going to heal their baby girl..."

The sorrowful silence that pushed in spoke the rest of the story.

"I'm so sorry," Dr. Jessie said as she reached over and placed her hand over Erin's. A few tears popped out of Erin's eyes.

"How could this be real?" I whispered. We knew these people, this baby, and their story. Their story was our story; we were living it together. We prayed for them so many times. How could their outcome be death while ours was moving toward life?

"Remember those Choose Your Own Adventure books?" I asked. "Those books we had when we were little where you could make a choice and turn to a page that would lead your story down a path?"

"Yeah, I remember those," Dr. Jessie said, her eyes squinting to understand my random question.

"I don't get it." I was still rambling nonsense. "Jack and Ainsley didn't make any choices that we didn't. If anything, they led us and we followed them. Their choices helped us make our choices. How is it possible that somewhere along the way...both of our families making the same choices, with great doctors and great prayer...why did their story splinter off to a dead end while ours is still going? Why does Faith get to live and improve another day while Mary Beth doesn't?"

By this point, I was pacing in our small room. "Jack and Ainsley did everything. Absolutely everything. Why? Why would this happen this way? I just don't understand."

Both of my hands were now resting on the edges of Faith's incubator. How could such gratefulness for her life and grief for Mary Beth's death occupy the same space in my heart? These two entities swirled into chaos, spinning my thoughts and emotions with them until all I could do was cry.

"Blake," Dr. Jessie finally said. "I've been doing this for a long time. There are days where the joy of seeing a baby finally thrive seems like it's coming straight from heaven. And then there are days where the pain of watching a baby slip away, and the grief of the parents, makes me feel like I'll never be able to breathe deeply again." She sighed. "And sometimes those extremes happen back-to-back, on the very same day."

She walked over and stood next to me until my eyes met hers. "There are no answers to the 'whys.' At least not the answers we are honestly seeking. If we are being honest, we want answers that make the loss make sense. And in so many cases, those answers just do not exist."

When I didn't respond, she continued. "Why did Mary Beth die while Faith is beginning to really take strides? I don't know. Why did my mom die when I was a teenager, but the drunk driver who killed her get to walk away from the accident?" Her voice cracked. "Why does anyone live while another dies?" She allowed the question to hang in the air for a few moments and then shared, "As I walked through the grief of my mom's passing, God showed me that so many times my whys just didn't have answers here on earth. And to keep searching for them, I was only torturing myself. Treasure-hunting for a chest of answers that simply did not exist. Eventually I had to let it all go."

I studied her sparkly pink cowboy boots, realizing that everyone, even the most joyful of people, carry deep hurts and unanswered whys. How could I have ever guessed that Dr. Jessie had known such pain? But it all made sense. Her own traumas had enabled her to care deeply about the hurts of her patients and their families, just as our struggles with Faith's medical journey had opened my heart to see the world through a more compassionate lens for others.

"I came in here to tell you both today how wonderfully Faith is progressing." Her boots clopped back over to Erin, and Dr. Jessie sat down next to her. "That is one thing we know for certain. And so we celebrate that. We celebrate her life, we grieve with those dear people who lost their baby, and we trust that God holds it all in His hands." Smiling, she squeezed Erin's hand and walked out of our room.

After several minutes of silence, I felt Erin's arms wrap around my waist. Through a barrage of silent tears, we watched our sweet baby girl breathing with lungs that were improving every single day. We thanked God for His goodness and mercy and, from the depths of our hearts, we prayed for Jack and Ainsley.

Over the next several days, Erin and I still struggled with the dichotomy of Faith's life and Mary Beth's death. Walking through emotions that felt about as steady as trying to hobble across slabs of ice on a late winter river, we agonized through trying to find the meaning in all of it.

In bed one night, I pulled out my journal. As I opened it, I realized I had been so busy with writing Faith's CaringBridge entries that I had not done any personal journaling in several weeks. The last entry was from my day in the chapel. I had written the words all those people on the painted green grass were leaning so heavily into. The words Jesus had spoken in Matthew 5:

Blessed are the poor in spirit, for theirs is the kingdom of heaven.
Blessed are those who mourn, for they will be comforted.
Blessed are the meek, for they will inherit the earth.

Blessed are those who hunger and thirst for righteousness, for they will be filled.

Blessed are the merciful, for they will be shown mercy.

Blessed are the pure in heart, for they will see God.

Blessed are the peacemakers, for they will be called children of God.

Blessed are those who are persecuted because of righteousness, for theirs is the kingdom of heaven.

Laying in my bed that night, I mulled those words. Words that seemed to speak beyond time and circumstances. I guess more enlightened people would call words like that eternal truths.

As I considered Jesus's words, I thought how so often we attempt to measure the success of our life, or our faith, or our outcomes in the wrong way. As these words express, measure cannot be based on good vs. bad, comfort vs. pain, even life vs. death. If we use those faulty measuring sticks, then we are declaring that those who live the longest with the least amount of pain are the winners, and those who experience great pain and heartbreak are somehow less-than-winners.

But nothing could be further from the truth.

Our lives are only made worthwhile and meaningful when we do the best we can to help those around us, despite our circumstances. This is a life well lived...no matter the outcome.

Closing my journal, I thought about one of my favorite Bible stories. The story of Shadrach, Meshach, and Abednego. They were three Hebrew men who were brought into a foreign land, Babylon, by a king named Nebuchadnezzar. When the king made a huge gold statue and required everyone to bow down to it and worship it, the three Hebrew men refused. Nebuchadnezzar found out about this and became so furious he ordered them to bow down or be thrown into a fiery furnace. The men still would not bow down.

What has always stood out to me in this story is the response these three men had to the king when they were confronted with certain death in the fire. Even though there was nothing they could do outside of denying their deeply held faith to change the outcome, they stood firm and believed their God could save them from the fiery furnace and the evil king. But their last words before entering the fire are where the real faith shows.

> *"But even if he does not [deliver us from the flames], we want you to know, Your Majesty, that we will not serve your gods or worship the image of gold you have set up"*
> (Daniel 3:18).

Jack and Ansley had that kind of faith. They'd stared into their fire and entered that furnace just as heroically as the three

Hebrew men did so many years earlier. As I turned off my light, I prayed that once again, Erin and I would be able to follow in the "even if" faith Jack and Ainsley modeled for us.

CHAPTER FORTY-FOUR

You

You want to know a secret?

I am going home today! I can barely get my words out because I. Am. So. Excited! After all these many months, I am finally going to my forever home where I get to sleep every night with my mommy and daddy and sister, where I get to have all of my meals with them, where we are all going to be together as a family of four forever and ever.

What do you think it will be like? Do you think I will like my new box? I wonder if I will have the same nurses at home as I do here? What will Rebekah and I do first? Maybe we'll go in the backyard and catch fireflies. Or maybe we'll run around with our dog, Beignet.

Zero Percent Chance

Or maybe we'll cook some hotdogs and eat them in the sunshine. Oh, my goodness...I just realized...I've never even felt sunshine!

These last few days have been a blur as we tried to prepare for the big trip home. There have been classes to attend, notes to take, prayers to say, new equipment to learn and nurses and doctors to cry with. And as we have worked through this to do list, there is one part of it that I've been looking forward to and not looking forward to at the same time. You know what it is? It's this right here: this conversation with you.

I've wanted to share this big news with you because you've played such an important role in us getting to this day. At the same time, I don't want to write this because I'm afraid of what comes next. What if we don't stay as close as we are right now? How will I do this great big old thing called life without you? What if scary parts are ahead for me and I can't tell you about it right away? Will we forget each other over time? How about we pinky promise that we will always be there for each other? And another thing that I keep thinking about is how will I ever repay you for all you've done for me?

Daddy told me once about this great big mountain somewhere called Everest. He said it was even taller than the hospital I live in, and that he actually saw that mountain sitting in his and Mommy's room back before I came out. If it was so big, I don't know how it could've fit in their room, but I know my daddy wouldn't lie to me so I didn't question him. He told me how he laid there and looked at that mountain and did not think he could make it to the top. He said the more he lay there feeling scared, the more he realized he was right and

You

that he actually could not get to the top of that mountain. That is, unless he found some people crazy enough to help him try to climb it.

As I listened to him talk about the mountain, I realized something: YOU are those people. You are the people that showed up and were crazy enough to believe we could get to the top of our mountain. You were courageous enough to stretch your imagination and let a preemie talk to you about her adventures in the NICU. You were the people that we did not even know were going to be there when we started to take those first scary steps.

And that brings me back to our dilemma. How can we repay you for what you have done for us? As we have thought about this, the only thing we can think of outside of returning the favor of prayer (by praying for you) is to ask you to do one more thing for us. So, if you don't mind, please allow your wonderful imaginations to grow once more and let's just see if this works.

We want you to close your eyes. Now, picture a child. Take a good look at that little one. As you see them, you might picture them in their PJs crawling to their mommy's arms. You might see that child taking their first steps and being caught in their daddy's arms right before they hit the ground. You might see a first birthday party, with a face full of cake and a mommy and daddy beaming so bright if you didn't know any better you would think they were glowing. You might watch this precious young child taking their first bite of big people food, moving from their crib to a big person bed, graduating kindergarten, participating in their first soccer game, attending their first prom, walking across the high school graduation stage, heading off to college full of hopes and dreams, meeting the person of their dreams, falling in love and walking down the aisle to be married, and starting a family of their own. Ultimately you might see this little child growing into someone who is truly making a difference in this world and in the lives of others. Now here's the part where I bet you are picturing that person to be me. And I have to say I hope that person is me. That sounds like a pretty nice life.

But that's not who we picture.

It's you we picture.

It is you who have been living your life up to this point full of ups and downs, fun times and not so fun times, and it is you who are now making a difference in this world and in the lives of those around you. You have given us the best gift you ever could—your hearts. When it might have seemed like there was nothing you could do to help us, you stepped out in faith anyway and believed with us. Prayed with us. Cried with us and loved us in so many ways. And if we had to guess, you are doing that for many other people too.

See, you have taught us so many things during this journey we have been on, but the one that keeps coming back to us is that despite the uncertainties life throws our way, if we chose to have faith and take those scary steps, no matter the outcome, we can still move forward. We can still make a difference.

As my family and I have looked back over these last several months, we have seen that when there was nothing we could do, other people have showed up to do what we could not. By showing up, they have provided that tiniest bit of faith, of hope, that we needed to take the next step.

We watched that hope come from a cleaning woman named Gloria who brought as much healing into our room as the doctors and nurses. We experienced it when a stranger took a leap of faith to talk to a grown man sitting in a child's chair in a toy store during Christmas and give him something much more valuable than money. Our faith was built when world-renowned doctors made us feel as if we were the only people under their care. We got to see how friends showing up with a cup of coffee and a hug can be as powerful as the most advanced medicine. We have felt encouraged to move forward by people we have never met who made us feel like family with two simple lines written on a CaringBridge post.

As this chapter of our lives comes to a close and we prepare to turn the page with trembling and excited hands, know that we carry you with us. We think about your journey of life that has brought you to this point, and how you have used your own experiences to bring life and hope and, ultimately Faith, to us. How you have used what you have to help us get beyond the hopelessness to a place where we could believe in something bigger than our circumstances. We love each of you more than you know and ultimately we want you to know how valuable you are and how much you matter.

"In the same way, let your light shine before others, that they may see your good deeds and glorify your Father in heaven."
Matthew 5:16

CHAPTER FORTY-FIVE
Faith

September 2017

My radio was playing Van Morrison's "Momma Told Me There'd Be Days Like This." The back roads of central Florida crawled outside my window like the tune coming out of my speakers. My windows were down but not to soak in a nice breeze because there was none. They were down to conserve gas. Hurricane Irma had blown across Florida three days before and caused such damage that almost all essential services were as scarce as the breeze. Gas was toward the top of the list. I knew I needed some soon if I had any hope of making it to the hospital.

As I alternated between praying and trying to find a distraction from my thoughts through the radio, I thought about how my mamma had also told me there would be days like this. Just twenty-four hours before, I had been standing in my kitchen asking Erin what was for dinner. That was when my brother-in-law, Ty, called me and said, "There's something I need you to do for me." When he'd said those words, something told me I should probably say no. And it was not because I did not want to be helpful. It was because sometimes you know things are about to change.

He then asked me to go to my parents' house to be with them because he needed to call them to let them know they were rushing Amanda, my sister, to the hospital. Amanda and Ty had been at Disney World in Orlando with their two kids, and Amanda had gone into labor while they were at Magic Kingdom. Going into labor at the happiest place on earth should have proven to be a fantastic story to tell for generations to come…if it was not for one small detail. Amanda was at twenty-three weeks into her pregnancy.

When Ty told us Amanda had gone into early labor, Erin and I knew all too well what that meant.

The next twenty-four hours were a flurry—getting my parents to Orlando to be with Amanda and Ty, rearranging my work schedule, and renting a car for the nine-hour drive down to Orlando. In the rush of things, I had not remembered there had recently been a hurricane; therefore, I was not prepared to find myself potentially running out of gas on the side of a random road in central Florida.

While searching for any signs of a gas station which still had fuel, my phone alerted me to a group text from Dad. Sensing it might not be something I wanted to read, I pulled over onto a dirt road cluttered with debris from Hurricane Irma. As I read the words, my own hurricane winds blew through my heart.

> *This is Ronnie. Thank you, men for being there with prayer. Both of our children have now walked that most horrible of valleys. The experience of possibly losing a child. God has answered prayers in both instances. With little Faith, the Lord carried us all and led the medical team, so now she is here with us and thriving. Today, God, as He always does, answered our prayers again. This time however, God said my Amanda's new little one, Foster, needs to be back there with Him in heaven. Foster came into this world yesterday and he returned to heaven today. I write this text through the most agonizing pain I have ever known, but I understand God is sufficient and*

He does not make mistakes. So I thank Him for all our Grandwonderfuls and trust Him only and daily. Otherwise this is a pain too unbearable to live through. Pray for our daughter, Amanda Chambers, and her husband, Ty. They have to find joy and peace after their baby lived only one day. He came at twenty-three weeks and weighed less than a pound. He just arrived too soon to stay here, but he was exactly at the right time for God's plan to unfold. Penny and I thank you.

I sat there in the heat of that September day, feeling as empty as the gas pumps. I had so many questions. Hard questions. Questions I am not sure we truly ever want the real answers to. Questions like, how could a good and loving God allow pain like this? Was it better for a child to pass so quickly or to be kept alive to see if the miracle of modern medicine could keep them alive a little longer? And at what human cost does that come at? But the one that haunted my mind the most, the one that I tried to run from the hardest, was a familiar one. Why is my baby here and Amanda and Ty's baby is not?

I did not want to linger on that question very long because I knew there was no good answer. I had taken that test before and came up short. So I put my rental car in drive and headed away from the debris-filled dirt road. As I drove off, those hurricane winds blew through my heart, leaving a wake of past questions and doubts scattered along the rough roads inside me.

Thankfully, I finally found some gas and made it the rest of the way to Orlando. Instead of heading to the hotel, I went straight to the hospital to see Amanda and Ty. Even though I had never been to the Orlando Health Arnold Palmer Hospital for Children, the setting felt strangely familiar. The smell of the soap was even the same, and it took me back to so many of my own NICU nights.

But one feeling was strangely unfamiliar. I was now the one on the other side of the door. The one walking into these parents' heartache. I was not sure if I was up for the role reversal. I did not know if I would find the right words to say. How could I do for them what so many others had done for us? But taking the strength I had found from those who had shown up for Erin and me, I knocked on their door.

Walking into Amanda and Ty's room, I was surprised to be met with smiles, not tears.

We visited for about an hour. An hour that both dragged on and flew by, like a movie your parents would make you watch when you were a kid that you assured them you did not want to see, but halfway through you realized you never wanted it to end.

I did not want to be in this hospital room, and I knew it was the last place Amanda and Ty wanted to be, but if they were going to be there, they were going to make the best of it. I was just glad to be with them. After my visit, as I was walking through the parking lot in the warm Florida night air, I realized I had never felt so close to my sister.

Arriving at a Walt Disney World hotel after leaving the hospital seemed almost like I was doing something wrong. Like the reality of this situation did not belong. However, being a Disney fan, I was comforted to know that when Disney World found out about my sister's situation, they had shown up with their normal magic making. They provided a couple of extra hotel rooms and several other perks that made us all feel well taken care of. That helped easy my feelings of guilt for being at such a happy place.

After showering off what felt like all the struggles of the day, I curled up in a bed surrounded by Disney characters. In spite of the situation, it felt good to be curled up in the happiest place on earth. Laying there, I felt so spent but not yet tired, so I opened my journal and looked back to the day Faith was moved to UAB. The day we were certain her time on this earth was coming to an end.

After my visit with my mom that day, instead of going straight to the hospital, I'd stayed at the coffee shop. At that time, I knew I needed to get out of my head and on to paper what I was feeling before I encountered what awaited me at the hospital. So with "normal life" happening all around me, I sat there in that coffee shop and wrote what I thought would be the first draft of the eulogy for my daughter's funeral.

> Is it really better to have loved and lost than to have never loved at all? Just saying that sounds cliché, but I guess that doesn't mean it can't be true. We have asked ourselves that question recently. We have questioned decisions we made and actions we took and wondered if they were the right ones. But we did not ponder those too long as we quickly realized that old cliché saying is true, and if we had the opportunity to go back in time, knowing what we know now, and choose if we would say yes to having Faith come into this world, we would say yes every time. How could we not? How could we say that we wouldn't want one of our children just because we knew it was going to be hard?
>
> I'm sure some would say that we were being selfish, that we were not considering Faith's feelings or the pain she had felt. And we would agree that is something we have struggled with. But it is hard for us to reconcile that with the understanding that everyone's life is hard in its own unique ways. Everyone on this earth will feel pain, experience loss and struggle late into the dark night with things we wish were never there. We have had our share of those dark nights recently. But simply said, who are we to decide for another person whether they get to live or not? That is not our place.
>
> Our place is to fight with every resource, every prayer,

every piece of knowledge accessible to make the lives of those around us better. To make them count. To give them the platform to stand upon so they can gaze into the heavens, feel the sun on their face and follow the dreams in their heart, and do the best they can to walk off that platform into this world. And while it seems hard to understand, we know that Faith's life has mattered. Even if it was short compared to what we wanted it to be, it mattered. Even if this ending is not what we envisioned or prayed for, we know that her life mattered. She mattered, and we are better off because she was on this earth.

Lying in the resort hotel, I thought about what I'd just read. I thought about all the people who had come alongside Erin and me during our darkest nights. I thought about the value of life. Not just of Faith's life, but the value of every person who has ever had the opportunity to take a breath.

I thought about all the people we'd met along our way, especially Jack and Ainsley and Mary Beth.

I thought about my sister and brother-in-law lying together in a hospital room not far from where I was resting, facing their dark night.

I thought about my daughter, Faith, lying in a bed far away, snuggling close to her sister. Safe and healthy.

I thought about how I still don't have full answers or understanding of the hows and whys of my sister's baby Foster dying and my baby Faith living.

But I also thought about something my friend Tanner's pastor said at the funeral for their son, Jackson, when his three siblings were born healthy and he was not. Their pastor had said that so many had advised Tanner and his wife Lauren to make hard decisions about their quadruplets early in their pregnancy. But Lauren and Tanner had not chosen that path. They had chosen the much riskier and rewarding path. That was the path of Love. They'd chosen to love strong enough that their children would have every opportunity to experience life. They'd chosen a love that was strong enough to not just hold the reward of that choice, but the risk of it too.

I thought about how choosing love does not mean things are going to work out in some Hollywood scripted ending. We choose love, even if the ending is not what we wanted.

With that, I closed my journal, turned off the bedside Mickey Mouse lamp and rolled over. Just as I was drifting to sleep, pondering again all these hard and scary questions life has for us, a different thought ran across my mind. Maybe the answer was not the goal. Maybe the response was more important than the answer. Maybe that response was something not so far off. Maybe the right response was much closer to something I was still learning so much about.

Maybe that something had a name. Maybe that name was Faith.

"Now faith is the substance of things hoped for, the evidence of things not seen."

Hebrews 11:1 KJV

Printed in the USA
CPSIA information can be obtained
at www.ICGtesting.com
LVHW090301131123
763661LV00078B/3283